AF703756

THE FACE THAT ISN'T ME

UNDERSTANDINGTRAUMA, COGNITIVE IMPAIRMENT AND BIPOLAR

By Judith Bridgehall B.S.W.

Foreword by Dr. Lidia Schuster, M.D.,F.R.C.P.(C)

RIVERBRIDGE PRESS

The Face That Isn't Me

All rights reserved.

Copyright © 2025 by Judith Bridgehall

No part of this book may be reproduced, stored in a retrieval system, or transmitted in any form or by any means, electronic, mechanical, photocopying, recording, or by any information storage and retrieval system without prior written permission of the author.

ISBN:978-1-0698569-0-6

Published by Riverbridge Press

Cover and Interior Design: Laura Boyle

Connect with the author: Bridgehalljudith@gmail.com

This memoir reflects the author's personal experiences. It is not intended as medical or psychological advice. Readers seeking support for mental health concerns should consult a qualified professional.

DEDICATION

To my dear friends, Cindy Metzner and Sandy Rysen, whose voices were always a lifeline when I reached out. Your unwavering support carried me through some tough times, and though you left us before I could share this achievement with you, those memories remain. This book is for you, a testament to the love and guidance you so selflessly gave.

CONTENTS

ACKNOWLEDGEMENTS

I am sincerely grateful to Geraldine Hewitt, and Iris Jensen for their generous feedback on drafts of this book. Your care, encouragement, and belief in its value gave me the courage to keep writing.

My heartfelt thanks also to Dr. McCloskey, whose steadfast support as my family doctor carried me through the hardest seasons of my journey.

To my friends who offered a kind word at just the right time, and to all who walked beside me along the way - thank you.

A special note of gratitude goes to Dr. Schuster, my psychiatrist for many years and whose guidance was a steady anchor in my journey with mental illness. I am deeply thankful for her continued support, feedback on the manuscript and for graciously contributing the foreword to this book.

Finally, thank you to those who continue to encourage me in my musical adventures. You have brought hope, strength, and joy to my life, and for that, I am truly grateful.

FOREWORD

By Lidia Schuster

In mental health care, we often speak about the importance of patient voices, yet we don't always take the time to truly listen. Despite my best intentions throughout my career, I know I have been as guilty as others of this failing. Our work tends to follow the rhythm of scheduled appointments-each neatly contained within the structure of a timetable. But healing does not unfold according to our calendars, and we often fail to see how much of our patients' lives occurs beyond those brief encounters. Just because someone arrives dressed and on time for an appointment it does not mean they are well: it simply means they have made it through the door.

Patient perspectives ground our understanding between the office and the outside world. This book serves as an important reminder that despite our collective attempts to eliminate the stigma of mental illness, there remains so much work to be done. What makes this narrative particularly valuable is its unflinching honesty. The author doesn't shy away from the realities of mental illness: the loneliness, the isolation, the profound disappointment when institutions and people we associate with trust and support fail us.

For practitioners: what strikes me most about this narrative is its reminder that symptom improvement alone is not enough. Our goal must also include functional recovery: supporting a person's ability to live, work, love, engage, and find contentment in the world around them.

For families and friends of persons living with mental illness: this book offers invaluable guidance on the importance of simply being present and listening. It powerfully illustrates how no one is immune from the devastating onset of mental illness. Understanding this can transform how we can support people we love.

For persons living with mental illness: this book offers hope. Mental illness and recovery are not linear stories with tidy resolutions. Within these pages, you'll find something more valuable than easy answers: the genuine possibility that with work, support, and time, life can improve and become meaningful again. Even when there isn't a cure, there is hope.

To the author: thank you. Your willingness to be vulnerable will undoubtedly help others-whether they are practitioners, loved ones of persons lived experience, or persons living with mental illness-not only understand, but feel less alone.

TO MY READERS

The title The Face That Isn't Me was inspired by my psychiatrist's reminder that I am not the illness. It is a truth that shaped both my life and this book.

I developed its contents over nearly thirty years, starting with times of deep despair as I sought to understand what had happened to my life. I would send emails to myself, record memories, create computer documents, scribble on scraps of paper, make journal entries and notes on my phone, disjointed attempts to find some solid ground.

The poetry I've included was mostly written during my darkest times. I wrote on my computer where the words seemed to flow unhindered. Pencil and paper were barriers to expression; the keyboard gave me freedom to rearrange words and lines until my pain was safely deposited into the document. Writing became both cathartic and healing, it gave me strength and helped me feel safe.

Over time, I was able to gather these fragments, reflect on the process, and write about the issues I faced as a person living with a mental illness. You now hold the product of those scattered notes, poems, and reflections, a record of my journey from illness toward health.

I offer this book in the hope that it will inspire soul-searching and change in how we relate to those experiencing mental illness.

THE DAWN OF UNDERSTANDING

The rain pounded down on the roofs and the roads, penetrating the dry earth and nourishing the trees, the grass and the plants. Slowly, the sound lessened until hardly heard, the slow pit pat of drips coming off the eaves troughs. Streets once deserted became active again with people scurrying about their business. I heard the song of birds and the joyful sounds of children playing, as they splashed through the irresistible puddles. A dog barked and the siren of an ambulance or a fire engine pierced the air. Behind every sound lives a story, of love, pain, hurt, joy, family and loneliness. At one time I didn't even hear the sounds, never mind think about where they came from. Consumed by my own pain, my own struggles and disappointments, busy in my own world. Were there others deaf to the sounds of everyday life in their community? No room for others, no experience of the struggles and joys of others? Not free to move out and about, experience each sound, feeling, touch, smell and taste of life? Sometimes I felt alone. Where did it go wrong? How did I find myself that day looking at a world not part of who I had become? How did the twists and turns lead me to feel disconnected, isolated and alone?

My twin brothers were born a year before the start of the Second World War in the United Kingdom. An ugly war touching everyone and everything in its path and yet life went on with babies born and growing up on bare necessities and certainly no luxuries. My arrival in the family happened nearly five years later in the middle of the war, my mother was thrilled to have a little girl. Although growing up I heard stories about my birth, for a long time I thought I was adopted. I never thought I lived up to the image of a little girl in my mother's mind and perhaps that belief triggered thoughts of adoption. I developed a close relationship with my father who had a more caring and less controlling personality than my mother. My parents went from a couple to a family during the war years and managed to provide well for their three children despite frequent fruitless lineups to buy clothing, the restrictions of ration books, and evacuees crowding their small home.

The government moved families from major cities to more rural areas of the country, out of the path of Hitler's bombs, thereby preserving as much life as possible. My parents' home was located in an area designated for the compulsory billeting of evacuees; refusal to accept assigned billets resulted in a court appearance and fines unless there was an acceptable reason. Two different evacuee families lived in our home for periods of time between 1939 and 1945. Two families sharing a small English semi-detached house with three bedrooms, one bathroom and one kitchen, in war time, presented quite a challenge.

At the bottom of our garden we had an Air Raid Shelter, built to protect people from aerial attacks. For years after the end of the war I heard stories about watching the 'doodlebugs' go over, wondering where they would do their damage next and heading to the shelter when hearing a "doodlebug" which indicated they were close. The characteristic buzzing sound of the flying bombs gave rise to the colloquial name 'doodlebug' a common name for a wide variety of insects. My dad was rejected for the armed forces but volunteered as a special constable in the local police force. When the warning siren went off, the blackout curtains were drawn, and he got on his bicycle to ride to the police station in the next town. Often the "all clear" sounded before he arrived, and he cycled back home. I don't remember much about my preschool years. Memories I do have are built from hearing adults reminiscing about the war years. Finally, peace was declared, the fighting over, but for many life did not return to normal; families were torn apart. bomb sites became playgrounds for children and rationing continued for years. Fortunately, all my immediate family survived the war which made picking up the threads of normal life much easier.

At the end of the war, life for our family began to return to normal, but the impact of those years remained. I started ballet classes which I loved and where I met friends who have endured to the present day. I do remember a few years later going out with my brothers and their friends on our bikes. They got cross because I couldn't keep up, so one of them would ride beside me with a hand on the back of my seat and push me along. Some friends owned horses, and I rode with them when I visited, took riding lessons and did a little hunting and show jumping but didn't take it seriously, fun but not a lifetime pursuit. My mother began breeding and showing Dalmatian dogs and I thoroughly enjoyed being involved with walking the dogs, grooming and going to dog shows.

About age seven or eight my parents bought a home in a small village, twenty-five kilometers away. My mother did not want to move but reluctantly agreed because my dad was anxious to restore this beautiful old house. My brothers now attended Grammar School in the town we moved from, and I attended a school even further away. My mother hated living away from her friends and did not plan to stay permanently in the new village. Because of this none of us changed schools resulting in a lot of travelling. Every school day my dad drove us to the railway station to catch the train back to the town we left. The boys got off the train and walked to their school and I caught a bus to mine. After school, the entire process reversed except catching a bus home from the station because dad was still at work.

Trusted to the care of my brothers resulted in me being at the mercy of the boys and their friends who took great delight in throwing me up in the luggage rack above the train seats and not letting me get down until the last minute when we reached our station. During the summer we all took swimming lessons and spent many hours at the local pool. Once again, my brothers considered it great sport to grab me by the arms and legs, swing me back and forth at the edge of the pool and then throw me in, I hated it but felt powerless to stop them.

The next house move marked a significant turning point in my life. After less than a year my parents bought a house back in the area we had left, close to the town centre and right across the road from the school I attended. No more buses and trains to school for me! Living close to the shops gave another opportunity for my brothers to bully me. By this time, they were smoking cigarettes with their friends but because they were too young to buy them, they made me buy cigarettes "for my dad". They used me for fun and to get what they wanted, and these incidents were the start of their abuse. Life did not go well for me after this move.

Within a few weeks, my parents out somewhere, my brothers and I together at home, the boys trapped me in their bedroom and raped me, a nine year old child. It was a horrifying experience as they took turns, one pinning me down and the other assaulting me as I struggled in vain to escape. I continued to live with those boys, silenced by shame, trapped with the horror, terrified I might be pregnant and not knowing how to talk about it. Most nights I cried myself to sleep. Sexual abuse, whether it happens once, or multiple times pierces the core of your being and turns the key, changing your life for ever.

LOST and HURTING

Dreams and goals
dashed on the rocks
by those
who only care for themselves
and seem to have the ability to deafen their ears
to the cries of those who hurt.

How do you feel?
How do you process the cruelty?
How do you find hope in a lost and fallen world as the cries of those who hurt are heard in the distance?
Where do I fit in the process?
Where do I find a place?
How do I know which way to go when there seems to be no path?

A year later was the Coronation of Queen Elizabeth ll. My parents were planning to go to London to see the event in person. They would leave the night before and stay all night and all the next day; my brothers and I were to stay home and watch all the festivities with neighbours who had a television. I refused to stay home, of course I was not going to spend all that time alone with the boys. As I insisted my parents agreed to take me with them and I had the amazing experience for a ten year old of staying up all night on the streets of London. We waited until the next afternoon for the procession of gold carriages to make its way from Westminster Abbey after the service. Sitting on the curb, I had a front row seat to watch the new Queen go by. It was exciting to witness history that day!

In the UK, the 11+ examination is an academic test taken by students in their final year of primary school, typically at age eleven. It is used to determine admission to grammar schools and selective secondary schools. The examination assesses a child's proficiency in various subjects, including English, mathematics, verbal reasoning, and non-verbal reasoning. I did manage to pass the examination to go to the Grammar School but did not want to attend the same school as my brothers for obvious reasons. Some local students attended an all-girls grammar school in a neighboring town which I wanted to attend to get away from the boys, but my mother decided "no" to me travelling again and my dad went along with it. The new school was not a positive experience, the teachers instantly connected me with "the twins" and their reputation for trouble. I had no idea how to handle what had happened to me or what to do with feelings I didn't understand and couldn't explain. Something different had attached itself to me and I couldn't get away from it. I was conflicted in who I was, where I was going, and what I wanted. I couldn't seem to fit in any of the worlds I lived in. Life in my family was traumatic, getting up to mischief at school provided some fun but frequently got me into trouble, church life was a strong draw but confused by the other lives I was living. In the midst of it all I managed to achieve some significant successes during those years. Through the local Girls Brigade organisation, I was one of the first girls to participate in the Duke of Edinburgh's Award Scheme initiated to provide young people with opportunities for personal growth and development outside formal education. Learning to wallpaper my bedroom, white water canoeing in North Wales, volunteering at the local cottage hospital, hiking and camping in the Cotswolds and preparing an illustrated survey of my hometown with local history were highlights of the program for me. I completed the program at the Gold Level and was presented with my Award by the Duke of Edinburgh at Buckingham Palace. On another occasion I was invited to join a group on an exchange trip to Germany with the goal of improving relationships between German and British youth. We stayed at a convent in Trier and toured places of interest in the area with the German youth and their leaders. At school I was made a prefect in the sixth form on the recommendation of teachers, probably more of an effort to keep me out of trouble than a reward for being a positive influence in the school! Prefects are expected to provide a leadership role in the school and carry out various monitoring duties which some of us did with dubious diligence!

Wherever I was and no matter what I was involved in I felt like a fraud. The puzzle pieces were all mixed up. I couldn't make any of it fit together.

At fourteen my dad passed away from pneumonia, a devastating loss not handled well at all. My mother struggling to cope took it out on us with beatings using a leather dog leash or a wet washcloth. I was trapped in a dysfunctional situation with two brothers who raped me, fought over food and thought nothing of throwing a cup of tea across the room and a mother who seemed incapable of controlling the situation.

Despite the trauma and challenges of my teenage years, I was determined to forge a path for myself. My resilience and high achievements led me to pass enough examinations for entrance to a well-respected teachers training college in London, England. After three years I graduated as a qualified high school teacher but my struggles with depression became more of a challenge and by the age of twenty-one I needed valium to cope. My professional career began with an excellent teaching position in my hometown setting up a new department in a Technical High School, developing the department and preparing students for Oxford University "O" and "A" level examinations. "O" level examinations are taken at age 15 to 16 in multiple subjects. They measure a basic level in academic achievement and were used for progression to work, vocational training, or further academic study. These examinations have now been replaced by GCSE's (General Certificate of Secondary Education). "A" level examinations are taken at age 17 to 18 after two more years of study and students usually took an average of 3 subjects. These examinations provided qualifications for university entrance or other higher education.

During these years I seemed more stable and was able to wean myself off the valium. I married a teacher at the school and after five years of teaching we decided to emigrate somewhere. Kenya, Switzerland, Australia, were considered; for me it was anything to get me away from the pain of my past and give us an opportunity to prosper in a new situation. Our efforts failed to develop into anything concrete for one reason or another. We then heard that a teaching colleague of ours was planning to emigrate from England to British Columbia with her husband and their four children. British Columbia seemed a long way to go but the idea caught our attention, after all if parents with four children would make that move, then certainly a young couple with no family responsibilities surely could accomplish the task. My husband and I obtained teaching positions in Quesnel, British Columbia, processed all the documents and began the journey of relocating.

The Past

It's all still there, nothing has really been taken away.
Perhaps my memory is not clear
perhaps hidden,
Perhaps the memories don't exist for me
Only for others who were able to be there,
afraid of the pain?
Was I ever there?
Part of me shut off from myself,
safe from the ravaging of who I was.
What's next
Don't know
Too much pain.
The courage to risk has gone.
The years went by, I opened up a little but
there it was there again, and I ran away.
The feel of leather on my skin, the wetness stinging,
left alone to do it all
no strength.

Confused, vulnerable behind the image of bravado, the wall of protection.
Never good enough, rarely able to come out and be.

Is it safe now to find out who I am

QUESNEL, CHALLENGES AND TRIUMPHS!

Much as we wanted to experience a country which we heard was full of promise, I wondered whether I would be able to adjust to gravel roads, hitching posts for horses and temperatures cold enough to freeze the inside of your nose. Would I be able to cope emotionally or would it be too drastic a change? I didn't want a return of the dark days of depression. Did I really understand how different it would be?

The project was exciting but increasingly terrifying as the movers came to pack the items we would ship to our destination; our car was sold, and we prepared to leave family and friends. In spite of the planning we had done for the practical aspects of the move, we really did not know what to expect on our arrival. I was constantly reminded of this by those who said, "Do you have any idea what it will be like?" It was beginning to feel that we were stepping off a cliff and I was desperately praying we would fly as we started to fall. What would it be like? The pain of saying "goodbye" was excruciating. Every part of my body and my emotions pulling against every other part.

On arrival in Vancouver, we stayed for a few days with the colleague, who was now settled, and purchased what appeared to us as a huge station wagon. I was sure that our accents and hesitant driving on the "wrong" side of the road were announcing to everyone that we did not fit in these parts, and I was extremely uncomfortable.

Mid-August, time to head north and into our oversize vehicle we loaded our canvas home (a small tent), portable stove, and the suitcases we brought with us. By the time we reached Hope(130km) I thought we had gone far enough for one day but, trying to adjust as quickly as possible, we pressed on and entered the Fraser Canyon. Fear gripped my whole being. The environment overwhelmed me with terror. The road twisted and turned as it followed the path carved deeper and deeper over the years by the river. It was extremely hot and very dry, and the vastness was something I had never seen before. I was not prepared for what I experienced as we made our way through the Canyon to Cache Creek and the Cariboo. The raw beauty filled me with awe, vastly different from the cute little towns and villages with hedgerows and neat stone walls we had left behind, we weren't "at home" now.

Once in Quesnel we looked for a real estate office and quickly found one on the main street. We went in to explain our situation and inquire about accommodation. Nothing was available until the end of the month but the receptionist arranged for a small holiday trailer, belonging to her son, to be hooked up for us outside a block of apartments they owned. This was a temporary but very welcome arrangement until we could find other accommodation. What an incredible relief! To this day, tears come to my eyes as I remember the kindness extended to us by those first people we met. We were welcomed by the residents of this new land; we were no longer alone, and one foot had safely landed on firm ground. We had met the first of what became a wonderful community of friends. By the end of that day, we felt very cared for, safely installed in the little trailer with a basket of blueberry muffins on the table, baked by one of our new friends. So much happened in a few short days, leaving home and coming to ... to ... a new community which I hoped would become home.

We soon purchased a house, and our new neighbors became our friends, introducing us to pizza, chili, hunting, golf, water skiing and helping me to understand that you do not HAVE to have a roast on Sunday! We had little furniture and no television, but they freely opened their home for us to enjoy. Brits are much more reserved; this hospitality was new to me, and we were so grateful for it.

We came wondering if we would fit in, wondering if we could make the adjustments necessary to be comfortable and stay. What did we find here? We found a barn raising spirit, rich in human kindness that flowed freely to uncomfortable newcomers. We were embraced by the spirit of the Cariboo in its people and Canada became our home. We settled into our new lives, thoroughly enjoying the experience.

As time went on, we made more friends, and acquired more furniture, including two cribs for our twins, a boy and a girl, who were born two years after we arrived. The transition from a successful teaching career to raising a family in a new country proved to be both exhilarating and daunting but made easier with a family of friends who helped us out.

As the children grew and progressed through the toddler stage, I began to see our son's behavior as more of a handful than most boys his age. We moved to Kelowna when the twins were nearly four years old and I was eight months pregnant with our third child, a daughter. I became fully occupied with a new baby and day-to-day activities, and our sons' out of control actions became increasingly challenging. A few years later during a visit with some friends in another city they told us about their son being diagnosed with ADHD (Attention Deficit Hyperactivity Disorder). Their description of his behaviour closely reflected the experiences we observed with our son.

This being the case we gleaned as much information as possible about the management of the disorder and with the cooperation of our now nine-year-old son put a plan in place to manage the situation in the best way possible beginning with the Feingold Diet.

The Feingold diet was created by Dr. Benjamin Feingold, a pediatrician and allergist, in the 1970s. It is designed to help children with symptoms of ADHD, dyslexia, and other learning disabilities. The goal is to eliminate food additives and preservatives thought to affect behavior including artificial flavors, colors, preservatives, sweeteners, and foods containing salicylates. Some common foods that contain salicylates include blueberries, avocados, mushrooms, cauliflower, coffee, and pine nuts. Once these foods have been eliminated from the diet for a while the salicylates are reintroduced one at a time to see if the behavioural issues reemerge. At home we all ate the same diet which made life easier and avoided marking our son as "different". We developed strategies to manage the implementation of this diet in as discreet a way as possible when he was away from home. For hamburger day at school, I would deliver a home-made burger suitable for his diet, if candies were given out, he would take one with everyone else, put it in his pocket and bring it home. I then gave him money to go to the health food store to buy a treat. Attending residential summer camp was more of a challenge!

A friend went with him and both boys went on the diet for the week! I took substitute foods for the camp cook to prepare for the boys, and it worked out. We all knew that the diet made a difference, and it was particularly evident when he ate something on the "no" list!

At that time little was known about this disorder, and I found myself trying to teach the teachers how best to fit him into the classroom situation. Some were more willing to learn than others and although diet and behaviour management techniques proved helpful it became a challenge for all of us.

Not long after this discovery my husband went through his own crisis and decided to move out of the family home, leaving me to raise three children with financial support from him but not much else. Financial support because I recognised my limitations and made it clear before we had children that we would either have children or I would continue working. We agreed to start a family, and I would stop working for at least as long as it took to raise the children. I was numb when he left, going through the motions of life, feeling as though the earth had disappeared from under my feet. As I tried to hold on to some control I would stand at my kitchen sink catastrophizing, creating a crisis and solving it in my mind! It gave me a sense of purpose and success in my mind at least.

I'm not sure how I got through those years, how I pushed through on the days when I had no strength, emotionally drained and responsible for three children. I had to find a way to become financially independent again, but the mere thought exhausted me. All my energy was focused on doing the best I could for my children, wanting to see them established on a path to independence and success. Periods of depression resulted in despair that I would ever get through this, never see a light in the darkness. Thoughts of suicide were often in my mind, but I kept pushing on.

Stepping into the unknown, I faced the daunting challenge of rebuilding my professional life from scratch as the single parent of three children, one who needed extra attention and care. At the time Kelowna had few job vacancies for teachers and I needed to look elsewhere for employment. After much research and several failed attempts to establish an income, I applied for and was accepted into the Distant Education Social Work Degree Program through the University of Victoria and on completion I worked as a counsellor, then went into private practice. The cycles of high energy and depression increased with the times of high energy being very productive for now!

The twins graduated from High School shortly after that. My son headed to university and subsequently followed a career path in the Middle East and my daughter left Canada to spend a year overseas starting with Youth With a Mission, based in Lausanne, Switzerland. My youngest daughter remained at home and then went to boarding school to finish her final two years of High School as I was finding life too stressful to cope with a challenging teenager. On her return to Canada my oldest daughter continued her education at university.

Sensing a new direction in my life I later took two years of Bible School by distance education and joined the staff of a local church, counselling and developing a small group ministry. My youngest daughter was now pursuing a degree, and the twins were working. Around the time of my fiftieth birthday, I went to a workshop on ADHD we had organised at the church. This workshop would prove to be a pivotal moment in my journey, leading to an epiphany about my own mental health.

At the workshop, as I listened to the presenter's detailed explanation, not expecting to learn anything new, I was struck by a revelation. The presenter mentioned a connection between ADHD and Bipolar Disorder, and suddenly, everything began to make sense. The patterns of high energy followed by debilitating lows, the relentless drive to accomplish which would inevitably end in periods of severe depression were not symptoms of a workaholic nature but of bipolar disorder. A window had opened, allowing me to clearly see the root of my struggles with depression. The illness controlled me, and I was a victim of it.

Armed with this newfound understanding, I didn't think telling my doctor my diagnosis would be well received therefore I consulted him, cautiously. I shared a few relevant symptoms, hoping to lead him to the connection I had made. The initial prescription for Ativan proved ineffective, prompting a more direct conversation during my next visit. Finally, the pieces fell into place, "It's all in your file!" "Yes, it is". I experienced the diagnosis as both a relief and a new challenge, as it provided an explanation for a lifetime of struggles but also ushered in a complex journey with medication and mental health management.

This started with Lithium prescribed by my family doctor. Thus began my path of navigating bipolar disorder, a journey marked by the difficulties of various medication regimens, including mood stabilizers and antidepressants. A referral was made to a local psychiatrist who was to continue my care for the illness, but that connection didn't turn out to be terribly helpful. I did continue working for two years after the initial diagnosis finding it increasingly difficult to cope. Over the next twenty years, I experienced the highs and lows of the illness, working tirelessly to manage it and striving to maintain as much normalcy as possible in my personal and professional life despite increased intensity of symptoms.

As the illness progressed the impact on my family was profound, straining relationships and isolating me from intimate family times. I always looked for a way out, never willing to accept my situation. Resilience, and determination to face each day, regardless of the challenges, became my survival. The path for the next twenty years went up hill and down, through dense undergrowth and prickly bushes, stumbling, falling, staggering and sometimes giving up for a time but as a survivor, I found a way out. I fought my way back, not always in the right direction but I kept going. I did everything I knew to look after myself, minimize stress and take responsibility for my own illness, working to be as well as possible. As I reflect on those years, I realize that my journey with bipolar disorder was not only a personal battle but a testament to the strength and resilience that lies within us all, even in the face of overwhelming odds. It wasn't easy!

NAVIGATING THE EMOTIONAL ROLLER COASTER

Living with bipolar is a roller coaster, not knowing when you'll be up or down, but we have a choice to allow the illness to control us or to figure out ways to work with it and make the best use of what we are able to do. Most people around us will be limited in their support; many people came into my life for a while, but most didn't stay. It's so important to appreciate the help and then be prepared to let them go. Living with bipolar does not devalue us, we are valuable human beings worthy of respect, encouragement, forgiveness, support, companionship, love. I chose to seek help when I needed it and to pick myself up and get going again when the illness overwhelmed me.

Bipolar disorder is a complex mental health condition that affects how individuals experience emotions. It is characterized by unpredictable mood swings, ranging from the highs of mania to the lows of depression, and can manifest differently in each person. There are as many faces of bipolar as the individuals who have it. Knowing someone with the illness does not mean everyone with bipolar has the same symptoms to the same degree as the person they know. Episodes will manifest according to personality and in varying degrees.

While everyone eats, drinks, breathes, and exists in similar ways, those with bipolar disorder feel emotions more intensely and broadly. This heightened emotional state can be confusing and overwhelming, making it challenging to manage symptoms safely and positively. They may feel the weight of their concerns more heavily, leading to exhaustion and difficulty in finding effective coping mechanisms.

There is no instruction manual for this illness, and it can be as disruptive as physical conditions like diabetes, where the body's chemistry is out of balance.

Managing the disorder necessitates understanding its complexities and recognizing that each individual's experience is unique. While there is no 'one-size-fits-all' approach, finding ways to cope with the fluctuating moods is essential for leading a balanced life. Successful management depends on recognizing its challenges and finding effective coping mechanisms to navigate the turbulence. A combination of medication, therapy, and self-care practices can help individuals lead a balanced and fulfilling life. By embracing treatment and acknowledging the need for a different way of living, those affected by bipolar disorder can find hope and stability amid the chaos.

The development of bipolar is thought to be influenced by one or a combination of circumstances. It is not the result of personal weakness or a character defect. No amount of will and self-discipline will make everything better!

Genetic Factors. A family history of bipolar disorder increases the likelihood of developing this condition. Studies have shown that individuals with a parent sibling or child with bipolar disorder are at higher risk. (NHS UK) Genes hold instructions for the function of each cell in the body, how we look, act, think, et cetera. However, because your mother or father has or had a mental illness doesn't mean it will pass on to you. Hereditary simply means you may be more susceptible to the condition than if there was no affected family member. The disorder can also be triggered by trauma and stress. On reflection I believe my mother showed symptoms of bipolar, and my son and one of my nephews both experience ADHD.

Biological Factors. Physical changes in the brain and chemical imbalances involving neurotransmitters like Norepinephrine, Serotonin, and Dopamine have been linked to bipolar disorder.

Environmental Factors. Stressful life events such as trauma or significant life changes, may trigger or exacerbate bipolar symptoms especially in individuals with a genetic predisposition.

Bipolar disorder causes major shifts in mood, energy, thinking, and behavior ranging from mania to depression. Individuals may be more prone to mania or depression, but most individuals experience depression more frequently than mania. Others may alternate equally between the two types of episodes. By definition a manic episode will last at least 7 days, a hypomanic episode at least 4 days and depressive episodes at least two weeks and there may even be stretches without any symptoms. What feels manageable one day may become overwhelming the next. The intensity of mood changes can vary from mild and barely noticeable to severe enough to interfere with daily functioning. The frequency of mood disruptions also varies, with some experiencing numerous episodes and others only a few over a lifetime. Subtle and confusing symptoms can lead to the condition being missed or misdiagnosed.

There is no way of knowing how your mood will be when you wake up in the morning, leaving no opportunity to prepare for what's coming. You do know for sure that the low will follow the high, you just don't know when! The body cannot sustain those energetic highs and responds by sinking into depression.

The episodes cause a person to think, feel, and act in ways, much different from how they usually present. I wasn't myself when having a manic or depressive episode but was not aware of it and when an episode had passed, I frequently felt uncomfortable and embarrassed by my behavior.

The manic phase of bipolar disorder generates feelings of heightened energy, creativity, and euphoria. Symptoms vary widely as it affects energy levels, judgment, memory, concentration, appetite, sleep patterns, sex drive, and self-esteem. Manic episodes can lead to extreme behaviors, such as impulsive decisions, reckless actions, and a sense of invincibility. These may manifest as driving fast cars, renovating the house, extravagant holidays, speeding. Whatever a person does goes to extremes! During a manic episode, a person might impulsively quit a job, charge up vast amounts on credit cards, or feel rested after sleeping two hours. It doesn't take many manic episodes to deplete financial reserves.

I often felt irritable, I could achieve anything, (however unrealistic), distracted and unable to concentrate, flipping from one thing to another with no consistent focus, and unaware of reckless behaviour. On the rare days I woke up feeling on top of the world and eager to start my day I knew that at any time I could be back to feeling depressed. The exhilarating, powerful, energizing times of mania made me feel alive, but they were exhausting, and depression was never far behind. Mania might be welcome initially until it gets out of control and extremely damaging.

Depressive episodes create intense and persistent feelings of sadness, hopelessness, and worthlessness, prolonged periods of low mood and energy. These episodes can significantly impact an individual's ability to function and enjoy life, making it essential to seek treatment and support.

At times it is incredibly debilitating, making it difficult to carry out daily activities and enjoy life. Unlike sadness or grief, depressive episodes are more intense and persistent, often lasting for weeks or even months. When depressed I've stayed in bed for lengthy periods, overwhelmed by the burden of my life. Depression for me resulted in a lack of desire to do anything, even the activities I usually enjoyed and did without too much difficulty. There was no feeling of pleasure in anything, just a negative wall, a great big nothing. I experienced prolonged periods of depression feeling like a nothing, living a pointless life with no purpose or future, only darkness. Life was not always like this, but at the time nothing would convince me that this would pass.

A mixed episode of bipolar disorder features symptoms of both mania or hypomania and depression. Common signs of a mixed episode include depression combined with agitation, irritability, anxiety, insomnia, distractibility, and racing thoughts. This combination of high energy and low mood makes for a particularly elevated risk of suicide. Individuals may find themselves struggling to manage the intense emotions and conflicting impulses, making it essential to seek appropriate treatment and support.

At those times, fortunately infrequent, I felt like the victim of a centrifugal force, spinning me around, totally disconnected and out of control, desperate to hold on to something concrete but unable to do it. The safe place for me during those episodes was in bed and asleep which I would accomplish with the appropriate medication.

I researched the option of suicide, eventually deciding in my more balanced moments that the risk of surviving with more damage than I had already was too much to risk. However, there were times when I handed over all my medications to a friend to keep myself safe. Thoughts such as "I don't want to live anymore" or "I wish this would just end" would often invade my mind and suicide felt like a logical solution at the time.

It's important to recognize the signs of suicidal ideation and take them seriously. If someone with bipolar disorder expresses thoughts of suicide, it's crucial to provide immediate support and seek professional help.

Understanding the link between bipolar disorder and suicide provides for effective support and intervention. By acknowledging the challenges faced by those with bipolar disorder and offering compassionate care, we can help individuals find hope and stability amid their struggles.

Not everyone with bipolar is unable to work. Many continue to function well however fluctuations in mood may affect job performance and relationships in the workplace. Managing bipolar disorder while maintaining a work-life balance can be challenging, however it is possible with the right strategies and support. Effective management strategies and appropriate communication can enable them to achieve professional success and personal well-being in work life. Allowing adjustments in work hours or remote work options can assist in managing stress and maintaining stability. Establishing a consistent daily schedule of sleep patterns, mealtimes and work hours will contribute to overall well-being.

Effective management of bipolar disorder requires an individualized approach combining medical treatment, therapeutic interventions, lifestyle modifications and support systems. Mood stabilizers and antidepressants are used together to prevent triggering manic episodes. Psychotherapy will address behavioral, emotional and cognitive aspects of the illness and help to modify negative thought patterns and behaviors.

Diagnosis and treatments are challenging, and medication needs to be closely monitored by a psychiatrist skilled in the treatment of bipolar disorder. Unfortunately, because of a chronic lack of psychiatrists, family doctors with an elementary knowledge of the illness are prescribing for patients. Treatment for bipolar is constantly changing and the most effective balance for each individual must be found and this can be stressful and discouraging. It may be necessary to try several different antidepressants to find what works most effectively and one medication may work for a while and then must be changed. The second psychiatrist I had would prescribe Paxil for my depression which took four to six weeks to become effective! Up to six weeks trying to survive the despair! It was never effective for me and after two months he would finally prescribe Wellbutrin which was effective in a few days and always worked for me. I prefer to trust the decisions of my doctors but really ……. six weeks of unnecessary depression was more than I was willing to accept. I asked him to stop prescribing Paxil which didn't work for me and prescribe Wellbutrin which gave me almost immediate relief. He did but I can't help wondering why I had to suffer unnecessarily. We need to advocate for ourselves or have someone do it for us because the decisions of others are not always in our best interest.

Medications may affect perception, and I was never quite sure whether I experienced distorted perceptions or not. Living alone precluded regular, consistent feedback I could trust; it was confusing.

Dangerous and exhausting as the alternating episodes are, at least I felt the highs and lows, medications flattened everything out to a dull life, none of the normal mountains and valleys. I resented the lack of feelings after being used to the high energy and crashes making it tempting to stop taking medications! There were periods of time with no symptoms and again the temptation to stop medications, but the price paid for this is not worth it. Proper treatment, to be as successful as possible, means taking medications regularly, as prescribed and attending recommended therapy sessions. Did I want to give up? Did I want to scream and shout, "it isn't fair?" Of course I did! These perfectly normal emotions need to be acknowledged before getting back on track and moving on.

Self-care, although frequently a struggle, is essential for the most effective treatment of this illness. I had to remind myself that my best was not always everything that was needed and be OK with that. I had to grant myself the grace to accept "less than' to keep moving forward. I needed to take care of myself by maintaining consistent self-care in my routine.

Conversations with mental health professionals and others experiencing the illness can provide greater understanding and mitigate the feelings of being alone. I found it helpful to talk about my struggles, but soon learned to make better choices regarding those I spoke to as it didn't always prove to be a valuable experience. I didn't need to be told that "Everyone has ups and downs".

Avoiding high stress situations, maintaining a healthy work life balance and using relaxation techniques such as taking a short walk in the fresh air, practicing deep breathing, yoga, or meditation can generate feelings of peace and calm. I did not enjoy any of those positive feelings spoken about following exercise and frequently it required too much effort. At least on the days I did go for a walk I didn't have the guilty feelings for not doing it!

A support network of friends, family, or a formal support group to encourage and help when needed, will avoid dependence on one person. Before my struggles with bipolar disorder, I saw myself as an independent capable person. I didn't want to burden others with my problems and would have preferred to cope alone but often I couldn't and needed help.

Healthy eating and exercising habits will aid in stabilizing moods as will keeping a regular sleep schedule. This is challenging when our moods are fluctuating however strategies can be established to overcome the tendency to neglect self-care.

At times I found the illness difficult to accept however facing the challenges and making the determination to function in the best way possible gave me focus and hope. Bipolar disorder is not anyone's fault. Acknowledging life needs to be done differently now and embracing treatment will make a dramatic difference. Few knew how I felt trapped inside a cage of mental illness. I am not the illness! Most didn't know the turmoil inside me because I frequently did everything I could to conceal it. I felt conflicted between wanting others to know I had the illness and the fear of how they would respond if they knew and how might I handle their response. This internal conflict exacerbated my feelings of isolation and loneliness, making it even more challenging to manage.

Life wasn't always all chaos there were occasions when periods of pure stillness and calm appeared unexpectedly, and those times provided a welcome break, some peace amid the storms of my life.

MENTAL HEALTH FROM SUPERSTITION TO SCIENCE

Understanding the history of mental health is crucial for appreciating the progress made in the treatment of mental illness and recognizing the challenges that remain. From ancient superstitions and rituals to modern scientific approaches, the journey of mental health treatment has been long and complex. This historical perspective offers insights into how attitudes and perceptions have evolved over time. Looking back provides us with a foundation to move forward and each decade brings fresh understanding resulting in new and more effective treatments in the field of mental health.

However, in my experience, the attitudes and perceptions of the public don't appear to have kept up with medical advances; attitudes of the dark ages still prevail in a variety of forms and those with mental illnesses find it difficult to relate to a world largely ignorant of the facts. Not only is there ignorance but frequently a lack of motivation to be educated. Believe me, no one is going to catch a mental illness by researching and asking questions! And that is the truth!

Attempts to treat mental illness date back thousands of years BC. Skulls have been found with holes chipped into them using crude stone instruments. The purpose of the hole was to provide a way of escape for the evil spirits believed to be causing the mental illness. Surprisingly, it is known that these people lived long enough after the procedure to leave evidence of healing on their skull! The supposed demonic was also treated with various mystical rituals, threats, and punishments but of course, all this was to no avail, but it did begin the process of seeking better solutions for those with mental illnesses. The Hebrews believed that illness was inflicted on people by God as punishment for committing sin and the priests appealed to God for healing, but the underlying cause recognised by most early civilizations appears to be demonic in some form or other. These erroneous beliefs have not been entirely eradicated by modern research and science; people will always choose to believe what they believe.

A change of thinking came with Hippocrates (460BC to 370BC), a Greek physician considered to be one of the outstanding figures in the world of medicine as it was then. He is recognised as being the "Father of Modern Medicine" and was the first to document two extreme moods which he described as feeling extremely low or extremely energised or excited. The Hippocratic Oath, thought to be written by either Hippocrates himself or one of his students, is still taken by new physicians.

Hippocrates separated medicine from its previous connection to theology and philosophy and established it as a distinct discipline. He introduced a physical theory of mental illness maintaining it came from natural processes in the human body. They believed that an imbalance in the humors (four essential body fluids – blood, yellow bile, black bile and phlegm) affected health and temperament. To bring these fluids back into balance patients were given substances to cause vomiting, laxatives to clear out the bowels, and were sometimes bled using leeches.

There has always been shame and stigma attached to mental illness resulting in incredible abuse. Mentally ill family members were hidden away in cellars, caged in pig pens or abandoned to the streets and a life of begging. The fear that mental illness was the result of wrongdoing or was even contagious, controlled much of the way victims were treated. Sad to say that in my experience these myths still prevail in the minds of some people today and many of our homeless are victims of various forms of mental illness and rejected by society.

The development of mental hospitals marked a significant shift in the treatment of mental illness. However, this did not occur until the 16th century when a few mental hospitals were established. Before this, individuals who were considered dangerous or unmanageable were often thrown in jails or dungeons, where beatings were commonplace.

Hydrotherapy was a popular treatment for mental illness at the beginning of the twentieth century. Water was thought to be an effective treatment as it could be administered at any temperature. Warm baths were used to calm patients who were agitated, violent or suffering from insomnia and these treatments sometimes lasted for hours. Cold water was used to treat patients with manic depression believing that cold water slowed down blood flow to the brain thus decreasing mental and physical activity.

Asylums for the mentally ill, when they did exist, were certainly not places of safety but notorious for the appalling living conditions and cruel treatment meted out to the unfortunate residents. Rather than centers for treatment they were more like dumping grounds used by ashamed families and communities to hide away mentally ill family members. Frequently patients were restrained with iron chains and shackles around their ankles and wrists. As better understanding came and different treatments were developed, this cruel practice of shackles was eventually ended and in the early 1950s, Mental Health America issued a call to asylums across the country for their discarded chains and shackles. On April 13, 1953, at the McShane Bell Foundry in Baltimore, Md., Mental Health America melted down those inhumane bindings and recast them into a sign of hope: The Mental Health Bell.

The inscription on this bell reads:

Cast from shackles which bound them,
this bell shall ring out hope for the mentally ill and
victory over mental illness.

Now as the symbol of Mental Health America, the 300-pound bell serves as a powerful reminder that the invisible chains of misunderstanding and discrimination continue to bind people with mental illnesses. Today, the Mental Health Bell rings out hope for improving mental health and achieving victory over mental illnesses. Over the years, national mental health leaders and other prominent individuals have rung the bell to mark continued progress in the fight for victory over mental illnesses.

Changes in psychological beliefs and practice did not occur until the development of psychoanalysis by Sigmund Freud, a pioneering figure in the field of psychology in the late 1800's and early 1900's. Freud believed that the human mind had three divisions—the id, the ego, and the superego. The id functioned unconsciously, driven by the desires for sex and aggression. The superego functioned both consciously and unconsciously, demanding that the individual deny the id's impulses and instead live a virtuous life, striving to meet society's ideals. The ego was considered to be the mediator, always working to find a balance between what one desired and what society considered acceptable. ("The History of Mental Illness: From Skull Drills to Happy Pills") Freud believed that anxiety arose as these three parts of the human mind battled each other, resulting in mental illness and that if the individual could discover and deal with the content of their unconscious, then their mental ailments would be cured. Despite the many critics of Freud's ideas, psychoanalysis was a popular method of treating mental illness from the early to mid 1900s.

During the mid twentieth century the prevailing belief was that mental illness is the result of a biochemical imbalance in the body comparable to physical diseases. Shock therapy was commonly used and surgical lobotomies, where the nerves connecting to the emotion controlling centres of the brain were severed; drugs were also used to sedate patients.

It was not until the Australian psychiatrist J.F.J. Cade introduced the drug Lithium in 1949 that psychopharmacology was established. Lithium is a mood stabilizer that works in the brain to limit the severity of mood swings. A series of successful anti-psychotic drugs were introduced in the 1950s that controlled symptoms. Valium became the world's most prescribed tranquilizer in the 1960s; Prozac was introduced in 1987 and became the commonly prescribed for depression. The introduction of successful drug therapies is one of the most significant contributions to the treatment of mental illness.

The first Diagnostic and Statistical Manual of Mental Disorders (DSM I) was created in the 1950's which broke down the condition of manic-depressive insanity (as it was known at the time) into three types: manic, depressed and other. Bipolar disorder was classified under "other". In 1968 the DSM II came out and manic-depressive insanity was changed to manic-depressive illness. The third edition published in 1980 identified bipolar disorder as a condition separate from generalised depression and established criteria for defining the mood disorder.

Unfortunately, the belief that all mental illness could be effectively managed with medication led to the deinstitutionalization movement that occurred rapidly in the 20th century. The plan was for these patients to be cared for in community-based facilities, but this plan was never fully implemented resulting in mentally ill patients being discharged from institutions who were incapable of navigating the processes of caring for themselves.

In 1948, Polish neuroscientist Jerzy Konorski coined the term "neuroplasticity" to describe the ability of the brain to change. Subsequent research demonstrated the brain's ability to change, learn and grow throughout life. Dr. Caroline Leaf is a cognitive neuroscientist with a PhD in Communication Pathology specializing in Neuropsychology and since the early 1980's she has studied and researched the Mind-Brain connection. ("Caroline Leaf Author of Switch On Your Brain - Goodreads") Through her work Dr. Leaf noticed that mental ill-health is not just a biological imbalance to be "cured" by medication; it is a disorder of the mind that may be caused by a traumatic thought life. This made sense to me as I was aware that my thought life was extremely negative and needed to change.

Dr. Leaf explains how our thoughts affect our emotions and our bodies. "Thoughts are active; they grow and change. Thoughts influence every decision, word, action and physical reaction we make. Every time you have a thought it is actively changing your brain and your body – for better or for worse." ("Who Switched Off My Brain? | Summary, Quotes, Audio"). Many physical, emotional and mental health issues today are likely to be a direct result of our thought lives. As we think, our thoughts are activated, which in turn activates our attitude, because our attitude is all our thoughts put together and reflects our state of mind. This attitude is reflected in the chemical secretions that are released. "Positive attitudes cause the secretion of the correct amount of chemicals, and negative attitudes distort the chemical secretions in a way that disrupts their natural flow." ("Robin Abrol - Positive attitudes cause the secretion of... - Facebook"). The chemicals are like little cellular signals that translate the information of your thought into a physical reality in your body and mind, creating an emotion. The combination of thoughts, emotions and resulting attitudes, impacts our bodies in a positive or negative way. This means that our mind and body really are inherently linked, and this link starts with your thoughts.

Scientific research continues with the search for a cure for mental illnesses rather than management of symptoms, but perceptions are changing slowly and there is much still to be accomplished.

MENTAL ILLNESS IS ISOLATING

Loneliness causes us to feel empty, alone, and unwanted. We may crave human contact, but our state of mind, our illness, makes it difficult to form connections with other people. Alone is simply a physical state of being by oneself, no one else around; a fact, an expression of reality with no positives or negatives attached. "He stood alone in the room" simply conveys the understanding that there was no one else in the room. Lonely, on the other hand, describes an emotional state, a solitary, companionless, isolated, state of mind. Now, there are feelings attached, and those feelings are not happy feelings. Being alone is, in some situations, positive and welcome, a busy mum with young children who have all gone to play at the neighbours is probably happy that she is alone for a while! Lonely is being alone and not feeling good about it at all; lonely is on the inside and is not determined by where we are, who we are with or not with. It's possible to be lonely in a group of people or alone and not lonely. A person is alone when he is by himself. A person is lonely when he feels isolated, abandoned or sad.

It is possible to maintain relationships and fortunately, I have some good friends. But there have been times in my life when I felt that I had no one because I thought people didn't understand or didn't want to understand. I was very much aware that I was not always an easy person to be with, but I needed that understanding from others.

When someone has a mental health problem or is experiencing mental distress, it is important to try to keep friendships going, even though those problems often make it difficult to engage in a healthy way and there may be times when they want to see their friends less than usual. It's incredibly hard to get the courage to speak to people and meet new friends when you're struggling inside.

Depression is a significant part of bipolar and a burden to be carried by countless people living under its cloud. It is the inability to experience pleasure, no good feelings around exercise, no uplifting feelings in the company of others at a social gathering. Then why make any effort to do anything? Much of what I did socially I did because I knew I should, not because I enjoyed it and many times, I didn't see the point and stayed home.

Those of us who've experienced mental illness need others, at times we may not want it, we may not know how to ask for it, we may push people away, but we need others. We need people who are willing to push past the illness to the person behind the mask and be what we need and that's a big ask I know.

Every so often I tried saying something to a member of my family about myself, what I was doing or how I was feeling, just to see if there was any response but there rarely was. I frequently felt as though I did not exist and struggled with the next thought which was "then maybe I shouldn't exist". No response to the real me, "I'm here, talk to me, I exist, I haven't gone anywhere". But I wasn't heard, the real me continued to be ignored and left alone to try and escape from the Face Which Wasn't Me at all. One long-time friend was able to consistently differentiate between who I was and what the illness was doing and saying. She would constantly remind me of the difference because she cared and knew me well before the illness significantly took control. Her reminders provided a strong anchor of truth.

Many people only see the Face That Is Not Me and relate to that, but inside I am crying out for someone to see me. When I did try to fit in the effort was overwhelming and the fear of not being able to maintain the connection was crippling. At times, the pain of loneliness became unbearable. I felt as though I was in a cage alone and there was no escape route. I think it was those feelings of being trapped alone with no way out that sometimes spawned thoughts of suicide.

There were few people over the years who picked up the phone to remind me that I was not alone. Victims of bipolar, for that is what we are, might obsessively make phone calls just to try and connect to some reality, just to be reminded that they are part of something and not alone. We, as people, are social beings and those interactions are so important to give us perspective and validation, to connect us with something outside of ourselves. There were times when I spent hours on the phone having created reasons for phoning just to have some human contact when I felt isolated.

Isolation and loneliness are common struggles. The stigma of lack of understanding and judgement is likely to raise a barrier frequently too challenging to overcome, too much effort especially in times of depression. The constant effort required to "keep it together" was exhausting and the fear of losing it and lapsing into inappropriate behaviour frequently kept me away from social events.

Healthy social interactions are one of the casualties of mental illness. We end up trapped in the quicksand of loneliness which drags us down and causes our mental health to deteriorate even more. I knew I shouldn't isolate but there were times when I didn't feel safe around people, I felt paranoid and threatened, not knowing who to trust. Afraid I'd wear out my welcome and loose the very people I needed and that has happened regularly over the years.

When we feel shame or are afraid of judgement it's easy to push people away to avoid feeling worse, but this only perpetuates our feelings of loneliness. Mental Health professionals encourage us to talk to people we trust but my experience has shown me that there have only been a small handful of people I could comfortably talk to knowing that I would be heard and still be OK. For all the publicity campaigns about reaching out to those with mental illness I believe it has for the most part fallen on deaf ears.

Mental illness is isolating. There were times when I was just not able to get out of bed; could not function. How do you explain to someone that due to the overwhelming weight you feel, you will be staying home today? How do you maintain friendships when all you want to do is drift away? How do you stay close with your family when you feel like your illness is a burden on them? It's all a huge effort and frequently I did not have what it would take to move forward so I let go and allowed myself to slide to wherever my feelings were taking me.

Having positive social connections plays a key role in coping with mental health struggles. We need to have someone, friend, family or professional. When the illness became more debilitating, I was fortunate to have a psychiatrist who knew how to keep me going in the tough times, never talked down to me and was able to relate to me as a person of value and not to the illness.

Because of the inability to maintain relationships my group of connections grew increasingly smaller over the years. The sad result being that when I needed a friend, I realized that I had unwittingly pushed many away. People move on and mostly there is no going back. When diagnosed with a mental illness, such as depression, bipolar or anxiety, our world is changed and we are looking for relief from emotional pain, as well as someone to care and understand. The emotions and behaviour of those suffering with mental illness affect everyone close to them. When I was depressed, I was not able to value anything positive; when manic I wondered what was wrong with everyone else because I felt I could conquer the world, and nothing was beyond me; at other times I was annoyed with those close to me which frequently happened during evenings of manic telephone use and I eventually realised that I was the problem!

I have learned how little people care that you suffer from a mental illness, whether it is a company you owe money to, the government or people you interact with in public. Even after disclosing my situation I was expected to handle myself just like everyone else. How silly of me to expect some understanding!

Mental illness frequently creates tension, uncertainty, stress, and significant changes in how people live their lives. People have different responses, but all are affected, and it is important to remember that no one is to blame when a person has a mental illness. Many have preconceived ideas, gleaned from news reports, experience, friends, jokes, movies, and various pieces of conversations. Beliefs about it being a weakness, a character flaw, using it as an excuse for something or that the individual with the illness is lazy or not trying hard enough. These views are hard to confront and painful to hear.

Response to mental illness can lead to division in families, serious disagreements, and possibly estrangement. This I know from personal experience. I don't think the response is intentional; more likely it will arise because of differences in understanding what a mental illness is and how best to deal with it. Frequently we feel misunderstood, "They just don't get it" or minimised in that our concerns don't have value or are not "real" and in my experience many people simply don't want to know, learn to know or be involved.

Friendship plays a key role in being there for someone living with or recovering from a mental health problem to overcome the isolation that comes with the illness. It's natural to feel helpless when a friend is troubled and most of us don't want to give up on a friend in distress, however difficult it may be to be there for them. I have outlined in another chapter some ways to stand with a friend or family member who is experiencing mental health issues, and, in most communities, there are people who will guide you in finding ways to maintain those relationships. Friendships work both ways and a mental health problem doesn't mean that you're never able to be involved in a friendship, to laugh or cry with someone else.

The reality is that we are living in an era of disconnection. While technology connects us more than ever, the screens around us disconnect us from nature, from ourselves, and from others. Wi-Fi alone is not enough to fulfill our social needs; we need face-to-face interaction to thrive. Technology needs to assist and improve our connection to others, not replace it. In this digital age, we have become less caring of others. At one time, our very survival depended on trusting and supportive relationships, but it really does not matter how much technology we have; emotional connections remain a part of being human. We need each other, not to hunt for food, for protection or to build shelters but we still have a need for human connections. That need varies with everyone, how deep, how many, how much, what kind, where they are geographically; endless combinations, all part of being human and embracing its differences. Healthy, positive people are wonderful to have around when we need to talk things out, bounce around ideas, solve problems, make a tough decision, or overcome challenges. Our need for social connection changes all the time and that is fine; each of us decides what works best for us and one of the most important relationships is the one we have with ourselves. We all need time to ourselves to rest, chill out, do our own thing, and think about what is going on in our lives.

Yes, people cause us pain, let us down, leave; it's not all fun and happy times but kept in balance the positives far exceed the negatives. We also have much to contribute to relationships, we have value, new perspectives, creative ideas; relationships are not a one-way street. We may have a mental illness but the person behind the illness is still very much present.

Social connections foster a sense of meaning and purpose for all of us. Mental illness makes it much more difficult for us to embrace healthy social relationships and not all social relationships are beneficial. Sadly, relationships with family and friends at times do more to bring us down than up.

Coming together with people in a community where we share interests will add normalcy to our lives and casual conversations with neighbors or colleagues will increase our feelings of well-being. Occasionally I went to a local Thai restaurant, alone, because I knew the owner and he always made me feel like a queen when I ate in his restaurant. He was so gentle and gracious with all the guests; it was a wonderful pick me up. Knowing that we are valued by others enables us to focus more on the positives in our environment and less about the negative parts of our lives. We will never get along with everyone but need to spend time with those who bring us joy.

So often we feel or are made to feel that we do not fit in, and the extra effort required to socialise is just not there, so we give up and retreat. The constant battle against negativity is hard work. People suffering from mental illness may not have had successful happy interaction with family, friends, colleagues, and other associates. Relationships may have been painful in family situations where young people feel trapped as I did, unable to get away from those hurtful relationships, nowhere safe to run to. These experiences discourage us from seeking meaningful healthy relationships; it's easier just to put up with the hurt and live with whatever situation we find ourselves in or we allow others to make decisions for us by default because that is easier.

Humans are born into social groups and live their entire lives as a part of society, so the social element cannot easily be removed from the evolution of an individual. We constantly need to interact and share our feelings with other people. Social interactions are vital for good mental and physical health. Those positive social interactions with friends and family make tricky situations and unexpected changes in life so much easier to cope with.

The challenge is "how do we get past the limitations of our illness to engage in and benefit from healthy social interactions". Cultural communities are breaking down, many family units are torn into different pieces to the point that we no longer have words in our vocabulary to describe some of the relationships in society today. People are separated geographically, my family is spread from one side of the world to the other, eleven thousand kilometres!! How many people now have hobbies they actively and regularly share with others? A dying breed, I think. Churches are another dying institution which used to provide vital social connections. An elderly member of one church I attended told me that she came for "the club" not the spiritual part of church!! Another local church has minimal attendees for the Sunday morning service but large numbers attending the weekly luncheon for seniors which provides participants with those important social connections. Young people sit around a restaurant table communicating on their phones with snippets of words, no communication of emotions beyond the emojis available on whichever program they are using. No observation of body language and I understand that communication mostly involves the use of an extremely limited vocabulary.

The world recently experienced a global pandemic of Covid 19 and the isolation necessary to keep the virus from spreading exacted a heavy toll on people's lives. Some were able to engage with others in a meaningful way, but many were not and even our best efforts were not always very satisfactory. The squabbles over "to mask or not to mask" only added to the stress!

Much of the time life is so serious with the responsibilities of work, looking after a home, and those endless "to do" lists, it's nice to spend time with people and relax. I have one friend I enjoy spending time with because it doesn't matter what we are doing, painting a bedroom, putting in a new toilet, floating down the channel on a hot summer day and realising we are sinking and need to abandon ship, going for a walk and having an ice cream, ending up on a black ski run which is totally beyond our level of skiing ability; whether everything goes well or we mess up we always have a good laugh about it. That's healthy connection!

Social connections require effort, either the effort to initiate a connection or respond to an invitation. This presents a challenge for those living with mental illness resulting in our social connections falling by the wayside. We may feel like doing something today, but will we want to do it next week? Consequently, our ability to commit to anything is extremely limited and I'm sure friends get frustrated with our lack of decisiveness, frequently not asking any more. I found that committing to events which did not depend on my attendance was easier.

Bipolar was my constant companion whether others were aware of it or not. Even when I felt I had it all together, even when I did have positive, people in my life, I was still sometimes lonely. Not always depressed but lonely and not able to articulate that to others in a meaningful way. There are billions of people in this world who live with or have experienced mental illness, and most of them have experienced loneliness because of it. People come and go in your life. I met new people, lost some and then met more but few have stayed. In the end, it is just you and your bipolar disorder.

Living alone there was no one there when the mania started to come on and I lost control of my judgment; no one there when the feelings of suicide were unbearable; no one there in the night when I'm home alone trying to escape from the inevitable. No, it was me and bipolar. After all the people go home and the gathering is over, there is still just me, and bipolar.

Feel the Pain

I walk away but know that You are still behind me
waiting for my return.
So, I return and risk again for a while until I have
stayed long enough and have to leave, discouraged and
disappointed.
This time will be different ..... will it?
Can I stay long enough for a broken heart to heal?
Can I stay and feel the pain?
Who will hold me when I hurt?

Will You still be there when the crying is finished?
Will you still be there.
The process is long and hard
Alone
The truth is harsh
Alone

But as I walk along the seashore
I hear You in the waves
As I watch the stars at night
I feel you in the dark
I'm not alone!

SHAME MY WOUNDED HEART

I want to talk and free myself of the pain gnawing at my soul. However, the thought of it evokes a cringing response driving me inside of myself to find some illusion of safety and respite. There is no respite and there is no safety, and I limp along until the next time.

The flower of deep longing for love is somehow hideously intertwined with the weed of abuse. Longings are wed to abuse, abuse begets shame, and shame is inextricably related to a hatred for one's own hungry soul.

Much of the shame I experience is due to the revelation of some perceived deficiency in my dignity. When my dignity is ignored or demeaned, I feel exposed as undesirable, and I will hate whatever part of me has caused the pain. The part of myself I hate the most is my longing to be wanted and enjoyed. If I didn't want, then I wouldn't care. If I didn't care, then I could not be shamed by others' rejection.

My resistance to trust is in proportion to the extent my parents failed to protect and nurture me as a child. My commitment never to be hurt again by anyone has created a hard, inflexible exterior contributing to the loneliness the hardness was developed to avoid. My defensive armour has added more pain to my soul and this pain has strengthened my resolve never to be hurt and increased the wintery ice in my heart. My attempts to protect have intensified rather than decrease the pain.

Shame has many facets; exposure, what will people think? Revelation, how will I handle it? Dread of consequences. To expose what happened is often more painful than concealing the act but the concealment rots away inside. I felt forever damaged, less than. The way out of shame is to talk about it and yet this is what the abused fear the most. Sharing these events in a trustworthy supportive environment frees the burden of carrying it alone and puts the shame back on the correct person, the abuser, and the journey of mental and emotional recovery can begin but taking the first step requires great strength. This sharing is helpful in a recovery group, with a counsellor, through close friends or a combination of these but the process will always be painful.

My personal experience of child sexual abuse is an essential part of my story. When I was assessed for payment of my disability insurance the psychiatrist made it clear that abuse was, for me, the trauma that triggered bipolar disorder. The deep-rooted shame of the event distorted my life from the core outward into every part of my being. Shame is one of the biggest issues resulting from abuse as it has the most devastating effect on the mental health and welfare of a victim. It's a powerful emotion. Abuse robs its victims of dignity, exposing them as undesirable, as lacking, not able to be wanted and enjoyed in healthy relationships. My victimization resulted in legitimate feelings of anger, hurt and disappointment. I didn't know what to do with any of it, no context in which to place it, no life experience to help make decisions and it somehow set me on the perimeter of the family.

For victims, shame generates feelings of inadequacy, self-condemnation, worthlessness, and vulnerability. For me "It isn't worth making an effort", "I'm no good anyway", "what's the point", school reports saying, "Could do better". Of course, I could do better but that was destroyed by the abuse. I thought my lot in life was failure so why try to do well at anything just to experience more failure. My parents encouraged me to be involved, to try new things which I did often with enormous success, but those successes never seemed real to me. I remember receiving a standing ovation after presenting a workshop to a conference of colleagues and immediately made it clear it was a "one off" and I couldn't pull off anything like it again! My failure in school was bottom of the B class at Grammar School, not too much of a failure when looking at the big picture but it was failure in my world, in the place where I lived.

Child sexual abuse is experienced as an assault on the self, negative messages are communicated that become incorporated into the self-image leaving the child and then the adult with feelings of being deeply flawed and damaged as a human being. The child is left with the feeling of being in some way damaged but unable to explain or understand the feelings that manifest in a variety of ways. Victims carry shame not belonging to them but to the abuser. This shame needs to be put back on the abuser where it belongs! It is like being sentenced to life imprisonment for a crime someone else has committed and shame shows itself in many ways.

- "Something is wrong with me".
- Feeling isolated and lonely.
- Fearful of intimacy or seeking unhealthy intimacy.
- Unable to get your own needs met in a healthy way.
- Punishing yourself with negative and destructive self-talk.
- Physically harming yourself.
- Suffering from depression.
- Compulsive and obsessive behaviours.

Shame will keep a person from disclosing and getting the guidance they need; maybe abusers know their victims' shame will protect them. It doesn't matter whether abuse happens once or multiple times, the victim will spend the rest of their life trying to figure out how to live with it. I didn't tell anyone for years. Eventually one day, when my mother was supporting my brothers in some dispute I had with them, I told her "You wouldn't say that if you knew what they did to me". I told my mother to ask the boys, and she assured me she did, the response "I've spoken to them, and it won't happen again". End of subject never mentioned again. On reflection I realize I did not and now will never know what those boys told my mother. I didn't benefit from the validating empathy and understanding to help me process and move forward, my mother simply did not know what to do or what to say. I had no one to talk to. I was scared. No one ever actually told me it wasn't my fault. I was scared, angry and helpless. My mother may have told me it wouldn't happen again, but I was never sure, and I lived with the fear buried somewhere inside me.

Shame as a response to child sexual abuse is exactly what is distorted about the victims' experience. Shame felt when we do something wrong or foolish is a valid response but shame for someone else's wrongdoing is not acceptable. It is important in every way possible to convey the truth to a victim, the reality they have done nothing wrong and there is nothing to feel shame about. Unfortunately, even today, in the 21st century, there are many who will express the opinion that in some way "they asked for it".

The pain of abuse has frequently caused me to be caught in the vicious reactionary cycle of either fight or flight. Both are my attempt to avoid the internal battle and escape my wounded heart and neither has been understood by others but usually condemned. Recently I was verbally attacked by both my daughters because I dared to make a comment about "musicality" in regard to playing piano. I was told in no uncertain terms I did not have enough musical training to comment! I verbally exploded and left the event, a classic response to being shamed, to having all my hard work, my training and experience dismissed as "nothing" and realising I was of little consequence, my family had absolutely no idea who I was or what my life was like.

Following the birth of my twins there were complications putting my life at risk. When I later asked my husband how on earth he would have managed with two babies and no mother, his response was "we would have managed"! Comments like this go straight to the root of shame, of not being valued, they pick up the energy of past shaming resulting in an explosive reaction of words, emotions, pain or all three.

My father called me Jill until he died. I thought I had used the name as a preschooler when playing house with my dolls but began to wonder about this when I started working with victims of abuse as a counselor. I had one cousin who was older than me and on one of my subsequent visits back to the UK, I asked her about my name change, how old was I when it happened? The response was what I expected but it still shocked me "You were about nine and you wouldn't respond to anyone calling you Judith"! If I became someone different maybe it wouldn't happen again, but I have no memory of the thought process I had around it, more than likely looking for a way to avoid the pain, to be someone else, to try and feel safe again. I was a nine-year-old child! Struggling with emotion I pulled myself together, pushed down the pain and changed the subject of the conversation.

Shame acts as a major trigger because when we are criticized or even given mild feedback it confirms in us our shame is valid. Anger is then frequently used to cover up the pain of our hidden feelings. This hindered my ability to learn, except in a manic phase when nothing stood in my way. In my senior years when I wanted to take piano lessons, I recoiled at the thought of fumbling at the keys with someone watching and approached the idea with a great deal of caution. I need not have been concerned as I am blessed with a teacher who gave me the confidence to make mistakes, to try and fail, to get it wrong and be OK. I am grateful for this gift which I still enjoy ten years later!

Finding a place of safety where shame is brought into the light, words found to express what we are feeling, recognising the triggers and reconnecting with who we are is difficult but a necessary part of the healing process. It takes incredible courage to admit our pain and our fear. In many ways it's easier to appear competent and in control than face the messiness inside.

Shame is a significant barrier to disclosures for children and adults. In the late 1980's I began counselling victims of abuse, working with adult victims of child sexual abuse and foster parents of sexually abused children. Counselling in this field was in its infancy, and I watched and listened as women of all ages came forward to disclose, most for the first time, their experience of child sexual abuse and the often-tragic impact on their lives. Attitudes are changing but there is still more needs to be done to provide a pathway for healing, surrounded by kindness and compassion. Victims need their friends and family to make the effort to understand, not to judge and react with harshness. As victims, we're trying but we don't always get it right and it doesn't make us "bad" people, we're hurting people trying to move on, trying to do better.

As a victim of sexual abuse, I felt shunned and rejected, of no value and this, unfortunately has been a place of sensitivity all my life, not worthy, not good enough. I've a great deal of practice in covering this up but occasionally something is spoken or done that shoots an arrow right into the core of the pain and it hurts. Thoughts of "what's the point?', "why try?", "I'll never be able to do it" come crashing into my mind repeatedly and I fight them off with adult reasoning.

I choose to keep fighting because I desire something better, I believe in the possibility of a life freed from shame.

A Picture of Shame

The waves of the storm
Crash in upon my world once again.
I stumble under the weight of emotion,
Stagger as I try to regain my balance.
Solid ground eludes me,
Helpless against the storm, lost in the waves
Good conversation, friendship,
loyalty,
trust,
caring,
intimacy,
Washed away by the waves of the storm.

I steal a furtive glance
I risk
Only to catch a glimpse of the cold,
piercing stares
Which confine me in the corner
where I have fallen.
Trapped by my own attempt to escape,
Disapproval is sealed on my life.

Once again, the shame is covered
and
I pay the price with more pain

UNDERSTANDING COGNITIVE IMPAIRMENT

For me, the first indication of cognitive impairment was realizing I was inserting words in my spoken and written sentences that didn't belong. I was too terrified to speak with anyone about it and brushed it off when someone noticed and corrected me. We often feel like actors and removing the mask usually creates more problems, preferring to find acceptable reasons for our behavior. At the time, the easiest way to cope was to bury my head in the sand but it seemed a strange symptom of bipolar and if I thought about it at all I assumed it was a side effect of medication

Cognition in the broadest sense means information processing; of knowing, perceiving and conceiving. Deficits or impairments are the result of a variety of factors, congenital or environmental. Cognitive impairment is evident when a person has trouble remembering, learning new things, concentrating, or making decisions affecting their everyday life. ("Alzheimer Disease and Related Cognitive Impairment in

Older Adults: A ...") Severe impairment may result in losing the ability to understand the meaning or importance of something and losing the ability to talk or write. At this point living independently is not possible.

Difficulties can occur with tasks requiring the use of previously stored memory such as learning something new, understanding concepts and reasoning in current situations. Planning, goal setting and the ability to work out solutions to challenges can also be affected. Lack of attention and ability to focus results in chaos within and in a person's environment, thoughts are not followed through, and task are left half done.

Mental illness is any disease or condition influencing the way a person thinks, feels, behaves, and/or relates to others and to his or her surroundings. Although the symptoms of mental illness can range from mild to severe and are different depending on the type of mental illness, a person with a mental illness often has difficulty coping with life's daily routines and demands.

I had to submit regular reports to my insurance company regarding my current status. One of these reports describes some of my struggles to survive, to make it through the day.

> *"Routines are just not possible. I do what I can, when I can, one day at a time. I have a housekeeper once a week to assist me in keeping my environment clean and tidy. A friend helps me to sort and deal with paperwork otherwise it just piles up and becomes overwhelming. I now employ a handyman to do many of the maintenance tasks I used to do myself. I quickly become frustrated and fail to complete tasks. I also have someone to cut my grass in the summer*

> *so that it does not get neglected and become another overwhelming task. My zero tolerance for stress keeps tight boundaries on my lifestyle as I avoid as much stress as possible. Many of my meals are prepared for me by friends. I struggle with finances and keeping track of spending which creates its own problems. I try not to think about what my life used to be like because, when I do, I feel so pathetic. These reports just remind me of all my losses because of this illness so I keep putting it off. Life is very discouraging because I frequently revert back to thinking that if I just make more effort things will be different, but I know that my effort makes no difference whatsoever".*

I would also purchase frozen meals for seniors, delivered to my home, making sure I always had something to eat, only needing to be heated in the microwave.

I had to use a phone box at the coast one time and couldn't figure out how to work it. The stress caused greater inability to think, and I couldn't figure out what to do or how to do it. What I did do was the wrong thing and the situation escalated. This resulted in someone being upset with me; more stress was created followed by increased impairment.

I remember going into the bank one day holding back the tears and saying to the teller "can you sort this out for me?" My mind couldn't compute the numbers and make sense if it.

Although I had a good disability insurance, I was desperate to earn a living again and tried many different opportunities, mostly resulting in a costly disaster of finances, time, or both. I couldn't do it.

I had great difficulty planning and carrying out tasks, such as following a recipe or keeping track of monthly bills. I remember having my granddaughters at the house one day and they wanted me to bake something. I explained that I couldn't follow recipes correctly and the oldest, probably 9 or 10 at the time, replied "That's OK Nana I'll make sure you do it right". And we did, great teamwork.

The impaired ability to focus on a task and process the information resulted in not being able to do many of the things I had previously enjoyed like knitting, sewing, reading and cooking.

What I found intensely frustrating was knowing what to do but not being able to do it. This became even more unbearable when people insisted on correcting me or launching into an extensive explanation of how I should be doing it. I wanted to scream and had to hold myself together and try in some way to escape. It amazed me how many would not be shut down. I would try to explain my situation, but it wasn't always enough and at times I had to walk away.

Away from my home I was afraid of getting stressed, not being able to think clearly, getting lost or not able to find my car to get home. Whenever I parked the car, I went to great lengths to make sure I could find it again by making notes, taking photographs or both.

My brain lacked flexibility, I found it difficult to switch gears from one process to the next, my mind lagged, creating debilitating stress again.

Getting to appointments on time became a challenge because I couldn't connect what my watch told me to the appointment time; my brain wouldn't go there. I felt foolish trying to explain.

Tasks requiring intense effort and speed were almost impossible for me as in playing a hand bell assignment with fast complicated sections in the music. I had to play assignments with less notes. How well I was coping with bell practice became a clear indication of the state of the illness at the time; in fact, my psychiatrist would often ask "How's the bell ringing?"

In November 2008 Dr. Latimer authored an article for the Capital News, our local free paper titled "Quality of Life in Bipolar Affected by More than Mood". I don't always read the paper cover to cover but I did read this edition, and the article reproduced below gave me much needed insight into my struggles.

> *"When treating a mental illness, the goal is typically to eliminate all or most symptoms—allowing the individual to resume normal daily functioning and to feel better. Bipolar disorder is no exception. In treatment, the goal is to stabilize mood and stop the person from shifting between the dramatic and dangerous highs of mania and the lows of depression. A combination of medication and therapy can often achieve this goal and treatment is generally considered successful once mood symptoms are gone. A recent study measuring quality of life in bipolar patients has now identified another area to examine when treating this difficult condition — cognitive function. In recent years it has become apparent that more than mood is affected by bipolar disorder. Patients also seem to experience cognitive impairments particularly in the areas of attention, processing speed, memory, executive function and verbal abstraction. The current study examined 55*

bipolar patients whose mood symptoms were either in full remission or at least dramatically improved with conventional treatment. An additional 50 healthy volunteers were also involved in the study as a control group. Study subjects were given a variety of tests and questionnaires to determine their perceived quality of life. Individuals with bipolar disorder scored lower in all quality-of-life domains than the control group and researchers learned mood symptoms were not the only reason. Persistent cognitive impairments also significantly affected perceived quality of life among bipolar patients. Even though mood symptoms were either controlled or non-existent, bipolar patients did worse than healthy volunteers on many cognitive tests and this impairment was associated with lower quality of life. Although this study was limited in scope, it is one of the first to highlight the impact of cognitive impairment on individuals with bipolar disorder. It also emphasizes the question of whether or not current treatments alleviate these cognitive impairments. Right now, treatments focus primarily on stabilizing mood, and we are unsure to what extent cognitive deficits improve as a result. Further research into this new area is warranted. I believe cognitive impairments are under recognized in bipolar disorder and very important. Not only do persisting impairments affect quality of life even for individuals considered in full remission, but they likely cause significant disability in work and other

> *settings. Ideally, treatments of the future would alleviate all symptoms caused by the disorder so that patients could function at the same level as their non-bipolar peers. This could involve newer medications or more targeted therapy than what is currently available. Only more research will answer these questions."*

This article gave me the courage to look at the reality of cognitive impairments in my life. I didn't have a cure but at least I knew what I was dealing with and could be more focused in problem solving. It reduced my stress and made it much easier to ask for help when my mind would not accurately and completely compute a situation.

Most can be significantly helped by pharmacological solutions for their mood fluctuations but clearly there is no widely recognized cure for the cognitive issues that for me presented a far greater obstacle to normal functioning than the mood swings of bipolar. The brain is controlled by your mind as your phone or computer can be used like a brain to turn the heat up in your home while you're still at work or switch the oven on to start cooking supper.

I continued to figure out creative ways to do what I wanted to do and be where I wanted to be with increasing success. There came a time when I was feeling confident enough to attempt travelling alone. A friend offered me two weeks at her time share in Arizona U.S., one week in Flagstaff and one in Sedona, as they were not able to use it that year. I spoke with a friend about it and we decided that I would travel alone to Phoenix, stay in a hotel there and she would join me the next day to travel north to Flagstaff. All proceeded as planned I flew to Phoenix, rented a car and got to the hotel. From there we both drove on to Flagstaff and Sedona and had a fantastic time exploring the area. We drove together back to the hotel in Phoenix, my friend flew home and the next day I had to return the rental car and fly home. I carefully mapped out my route to the airport car rental and headed out onto a busy freeway. I saw the sign to turn off the freeway but couldn't get into the lane to exit and had to keep going to who knows where. Now I was lost and stressed on a busy freeway! I fixed my mind on the next step which was to get off the freeway which I managed to do some distance later and pulled off to try and figure out where I was and how to get to where I needed to be! During this process I decided that if I couldn't find my way I would call a cab and follow it to the airport car rental! Phew! I had a backup plan! There was no GPS back then, so I was using a paper map and had to keep stopping to check the map, but I did get the car returned with plenty of time to catch the flight home. A successful adventure with enough support to give me the confidence I needed to travel again. An important key to managing the stress was to plan ahead, create back up plans and have reasonable expectations.

Despite the trauma and hardships, I have found ways to navigate the complexities of mental illness, seeking help, and embracing the support of friends and professionals. As I reflect on my experiences, I am reminded that while the path may be fraught with obstacles, it is also filled with moments of triumph and hope. This journey has taught me that we are not defined by our struggles but by how we choose to face them, and in doing so, we can find a sense of peace and purpose.

THE MANY FACES OF VICTIMIZATION

Mental illness holds within it many avenues of victimization, discrimination, abuse, exploitation, misunderstanding and stigma. Bipolar illness is The Face That Isn't Me. The real me is aching to be acknowledged but some only view the illness, and others don't notice anything at all. My IQ didn't change, my interests didn't change, my need for relationship didn't change but the victimization because of mental illness at times choked out the real me, failing to acknowledge me. In the midst of it all we still have choices, and I chose to stand tall whenever I was able and not be swallowed up by the negative behaviour of others.

Individuals with mental illnesses are among the most marginalized, oppressed, devalued and stigmatized populations in our society. Socially the losses are great for someone with a mental illness, partly due to unjust social structures. At times we behave in ways not considered "normal", logical or understandable, which can leave us isolated in social situations. I was fortunate to have a few friends who did their homework and were able to understand and relate to me when the illness reared its ugly head. Most back away from what they don't understand, and victims of mental illness are frequently left to fend for themselves. We are who we are, we are not the illness and who we are is repeatedly lost to those around us.

Having my quality of life destroyed by bipolar was devastating, I did nothing to cause the illness and there was nothing I could have done to stop it, and this victimization needs to stop now.

Individuals with mental illness are victimized in many ways. This frequently involves acts such as theft of clothing or money but also includes assault, rape, or being killed. Women who have a severe psychiatric disorder are especially vulnerable. While these situations do occur, it is more frequently that we endure being ignored and not respected in less overt communications. I was once told "you just use your illness as an excuse to get out of things you don't feel like doing". Many times, my hurt and frustration reached the point where I wanted to lash out but couldn't find an acceptable way of expressing how I felt. Trapped in the cage of this illness I often felt helpless and out of control.

Victims of mental illness suffer abuse in many ways, not believed, unable to access services, unable to complete tasks expected of them by others. Pain, hurt, anger and more pain, hurt and anger. And then the self-righteous in the public blame violence on mental illness! I felt I lost all credibility with my family after I was diagnosed, an attitude that continued after I was healed and free of any symptoms. They shot down my input and invalidated my knowledge and opinions. How different it might have been had I been able to continue my professional life and my place in the family rather than being depressed or manic, not working and not acceptable in the family unit?

I underwent experiences where I was taken advantage of, although at the time I did not fully understand the extent of the situation. As an empath with a mental health condition I was the perfect victim! This dynamic often resulted in my concerns being dismissed, as credibility was frequently granted to those who were more persuasive and charismatic, leaving me susceptible to blame. People with mental health issues are targeted more often because they are seen as vulnerable and easier to manipulate. Individuals experiencing anxiety, depression, or low self-esteem may exhibit increased vulnerability to the initial appeal, intense attention, and subsequent controlling behaviors of others. A person with narcissistic traits thrives on dominance and validation, and someone with mental health challenges may already question their self-worth, making it easier for others to gaslight, guilt trip, or isolate them. This dynamic can be especially harmful because it reinforces the victims' struggles while giving the other person a sense of power.

If I was sick and needy all was well, I was a steady and reliable source of supply but once I was healed and began to recognize the people with narcissistic traits lurking in my relationships it all went wrong, and they turned on me in the most cruel of ways. Awareness is the key. People with mental health challenges can build strong boundaries, seek support, and recognize red flags early to avoid falling into these toxic cycles. Fortunately, I was able to either end or distance those relationships but the devastation of realising how I was used and manipulated almost destroyed me.

Stigma is a set of negative and usually untrue beliefs society holds about someone or something. It affects the thoughts and feelings about certain health conditions.

Stigma relates to the way society views and acts and how we feel about ourselves. "Stigma happens when a person defines someone by their illness rather than who they are as an individual." ("What is mental health stigma examples? - Wellbeing Port") For example, they might be labelled 'psychotic' rather than 'a person experiencing psychosis' or labelled 'bipolar' rather than 'a person with bipolar disorder'.

Self-stigma happens when someone starts to internalize the negative views society holds about them. These negative attitudes are hurtful for anyone with a health condition, making a person's mental, physical, and social well-being even worse.

Bipolar is generally misunderstood and the stigmatism surrounding it is mostly due to a lack of knowledge and understanding of the illness. It changes every aspect of a person's life, everything from work to relationships is affected by it and it has an enormous impact on the everyday productivity of a sufferer. I believe the stigma surrounding mental health is often the reason the subject is ignored. For many, mental illness is seen as a sign of weakness. Maybe mental illness should be renamed in some way to reflect its true nature and remove at least some of the stigma around the illnesses.

Those struggling with mental illness are at times blamed by society for their current situations, with no attention paid to the socio-political context influencing their experiences. Common stereotypes presenting people with mental illness as dangerous, volatile, unkempt and worthless are sometimes fuelled by the media and each time the media reports in this way it makes it more difficult to talk about their illness. I believe the media plays a key role in perpetuating stereotypes and shaping public opinion and it is important to balance reporting on mental health, to include the broader context of the situation.

When someone treats you in a negative way because of your mental illness, this is discrimination. Individuals with bipolar disorder are at times, by some, depicted in an out-of-control, dangerous, and manic state while most with bipolar disorder spend much of their time depressed. I was once referred to a "loose cannon" a figurative expression that describes a person who is uncontrollable and likely to cause problems or embarrassment due to their unpredictable or rash behaviour.

Assumptions about how someone's condition affects them, and their behavior should not be made because two people both diagnosed with bipolar disorder will have some similar but other distinctly different experiences.

My children were young adults by the time the illness became a problem, and it must have been confusing and stressful for them. They chose to withdraw and for many years I was not included in family celebrations and not allowed to spend time with my two grandsons. Their mother didn't want me in and out of their lives emotionally even though I had regular contact with my granddaughters without any problems. The girls grew up understanding the illness as was age appropriate and we were able to have a positive relationship. I regularly babysat them and took them to after school activities. My oldest daughter continued contact but did not engage with me personally except to arrange time with the girls. A major difficulty for me was not being told about things going on in the family, not being part of the process and then having a major change dropped on me, when I was unprepared. There were occasions when I found out what was going on from others and had to deal with the hurt of rejection rather than being respected enough to be part of the process. Sometimes being left out is harder to handle than dealing with the situation. All incredibly confusing for me. To this day there is an unspoken, but for me a real sense of being on the outside of my family, of differing beliefs, realities, priorities and perspectives regularly clashing in a hurtful way.

The hurt is often caused by ignorance and, despite all the effort to educate our generation about mental illness, the fears and misunderstanding remain. I once heard a sermon, in my home church at the time, explaining that Saul probably had bipolar which accounted for his murderous nature. Sitting in the congregation I now felt branded, not only by mental illness, but also with a murderous nature because I had been diagnosed with bipolar. How far have we come from the insane asylums of the past? We don't lock people up anymore because they have a mental illness, but families and friends walk away and some victims of mental illness end up with no family, no friends, no job and, at times, no home. Fear of being labelled as having a mental health problem also reduces the likelihood of individuals with mental health disorders seeking treatment. Stigma and prejudice contribute to the fundamental abuse of human rights and sadly continues to be seen in some of our communities. There is a lack of qualified mental health workers which results in doctors, nurses, police, and other community workers being faced with issues they are not qualified or experienced to help; consequently vulnerable individuals do not receive what they need.

I was hurt, damaged and suffered because of the actions of others and because of mental illness but I still knew to choose how to move forward even though putting the choices into action was often one step forward and two steps back! I could choose positive or negative, choose to hope or despair, try to move forward the best way possible or stay stuck. Positive choices are hard to make when the illness throws you into extended periods of depression and I spent plenty of time in despair as many of my poems reflect. I could blame my brothers for the trauma they inflicted, but I chose to forgive, and I chose not to stay in the pit of blame and despair, I chose to try and find a better life. I chose to make lemonade out of the sour lemons. I chose to find and climb a ladder out of the pit, falling back down many times but getting up again and putting one foot on the first rung. Perhaps I never accepted the illness, I kept fighting. I was able to faithfully take my medication and at times problem solve the deficits in my brain function; but what I couldn't do was control the victimization by family, society, friends, systems, churches and other organizations. This was re-victimization because of the illness, and it affects all aspects of life, limiting access to employment and housing, harming social relationships and reducing self-esteem. For me being a victim meant accepting the victimization and giving up and I couldn't give up.

BROKEN TRUST

The church is supposed to be a sanctuary, a place of refuge and support. Yet, as I navigated the labyrinth of deceit and negligence within its walls, I found myself trapped in a web of betrayal.

Criminal Record Checks were expected of all individuals working with the youth at the church, the forms were completed and passed to the administrator for processing by the RCMP (at no cost to the church) but the administrator did not follow through with sending the forms. Instead, he chose to store them in his filing cabinet and deprived our youth of the protection of knowing there were no known child offenders working with the children and youth attending church programs. I uncovered this when I received a request from a social worker in the community involving the criminal record checks and advised the senior pastor of what I had discovered. His response was chillingly indifferent: "Mind your own business." This was the beginning of my disillusionment, a journey through the dark corridors of an institution that had failed its most vulnerable members. To keep quiet meant lying in response to the social worker which I could not and would not do. I had an obligation both spiritually and professionally to be honest and tell the various youth leaders their workers had not been screened.

My vehicle was involved in a hit and run incident in the church parking lot. Several months later, I discovered the senior pastor of the church had caused the damage. He did not acknowledge it until confronted, at which point he offered to pay my deductible but as far as I am aware left the Provincial Insurance Corporation to pay the balance. Where was the integrity?

There was an accident involving our church van, twelve youths, and an inexperienced driver with summer tires on a dangerous winter highway. No criminal charges were laid as the tires were not the issue; however, the irresponsibility of this situation was shocking. I debriefed the shaken group when they returned home, fortunately without serious injuries. The leadership's main concern was to keep the incident quiet.

I was incredibly confused and conflicted by all of this. As a member of the church staff, I was expected to stand by the other members of the team but how could I condone this reckless behaviour which put others at risk with no clarity of right and wrong and no consideration of integrity. I was not coping well, and the stress was affecting my illness.

I talked this situation through with my doctor and he suggested a period of absence from my work at the church. He communicated to the church in writing that I was "ill and cannot work at this time. Return to work is uncertain at this point." What developed for me over the next few weeks was what I now understand was a mixture of mania and depression, extreme agitation, anxiety, fatigue, guilt, impulsiveness, irritability, suicidal ideation, panic, paranoia and rage occurring simultaneously. I had no idea what was happening to me, my psychiatrist was nowhere to be found, and I was incapable of communicating rationally. During my sick leave senior ministry staff and their secretary harassed me with telephone calls I was not well enough to answer and refused to accept my daughters' explanations and offer of help, in fact they refused to have a conversation with her! They would not accept I was not well and not capable of a meeting with them. The arrogance and lack of integrity of those men was hard to fathom!

Church is a tough place for anyone with depression, anxiety, bipolar, or any other mental disorder because most church members don't know how to care for them and don't make the effort to be educated. Depression is difficult to understand if you've never experienced the feelings of loneliness, hopelessness, and shame. Bipolar doesn't fit into any sort of neat category. It's hard to know how to effectively care for a person who is mired in the darkness. It's not as simple as dealing with a headache or the flu, where there is a clear cause and a clear cure. Most churches have nothing to offer and frequently feel impotent when they meet the illness face to face but as Christians, we are called to bear one another's burdens, even if we don't totally understand the burden. We're called to lift one another up, to strengthen one another, and to shower the love of God on one another. Church should be the safest place for those with a mental illness. It should be a place of refuge amidst the constant misery of the illness.

Not for me, my illness escalated to where I was incapable of organizing coherent thought or managing my personal care but the church, in their ignorance, demanded I return to work on a certain date or action would be taken.

My doctors note explaining I was ill and not able to be at work and my daughter's intervention were ignored and when I didn't arrive for work, on the date decided by the church, termination papers were delivered to my door by courier. Traumatized by my illness and disconnected from my psychiatrist, the church made things worse. Thankfully, my son-in-law was home and supported me through that difficult day. I lost my ministry, my income, my social connections and not an offer of prayer was in sight! I've heard churches shoot their wounded and I found it to be true, in my situation. This church had been more than happy for me to start an incredibly successful Support Group Ministry; to be published in the National Church Magazine; speak at the National Women's Conference and share as a guest on a National Christian Television Program but cast me out and treated me like a pariah when I was no longer able to function because of a mental illness and the additional stress of seeing so much wrongdoing among the leadership. More mental illness education is important and necessary in our churches. The leadership of my church had been aware of my bipolar diagnosis from the beginning, I took the risk to disclose my diagnosis to the senior pastor, as soon as I received it, fully expecting his understanding as according to him, a member of his own family experienced the same condition. Sadly, not one of the pastors or my colleagues at the church had the courage to be there for me or my family.

My reputation was marred by insensitivity and disregard for Employment Standards and Human Rights, not to mention Scriptural standards for church operations and plain "telling the truth". The situation was straightforward. I was on legitimate sick leave, and they fired me, and the church leadership had to face the consequences of their decisions, a simple apology would have ended the entire process, but there was nothing but lies and cover up.

As my mood later stabilized my first recourse was to contact Human Rights regarding the firing of an employee when on sick leave. "The employee's job is protected while they're on a leave of absence: Employment is considered to be continuous. ("Handling absences and other disruptions - Gov") The employee receives wage and benefit increases as usual. You can't fire or lay off the employee or change the job conditions unless they agree in writing." ("Handling absences and other disruptions - Gov") The law is for the lawless and I chose to go to law over these issues as soon as I was emotionally and cognitively able. I have always been concerned for anyone who is not able to take proper action when wronged, for whatever reason, and believe if you can you should. Senior ministry staff acted as though they were above the law, totally without compassion, and it was important for them to realize the law is our teacher and necessary for us all. The process of Human Rights Assessments was backed up and it was suggested I pursue a civil resolution through the courts. It's my understanding that under Human Rights Law, you can't be discriminated against at work because of a mental disability.

I may have been a victim of misrepresentations to the board by senior ministry staff. Possibly the board were not made aware of all the information relating to my sick leave, only what the senior pastor chose to pass on. He had received the written memo from my doctor which, I understand, was not passed on. Upon receipt of the memo from my doctor, further discussion and harassment should have ceased. Instead, arrangements should have been made to facilitate my return to work at a suitable time. In fact, there were several opportunities in the process when the church ministry team could have done the honorable thing but made a choice to continue in their deception and their hurtful behavior. A group of friends tried to speak with the leadership, but they were not heard. One deacon spent time with me to find out the truth of what had happened and spoke up, but he was ostracized and I'm told he was turned away from the church doors and not even allowed to enter the building for services with his family. There were two elderly gentlemen in the congregation who reached out to me and kept regular prayerful contact throughout, an appreciated example of Godly behaviour.

I'm thankful to have found a patient and focused lawyer who worked through the challenges of my mental illness to ensure justice was served. The efforts of leadership to try and prove I was terminated with cause were quite irrelevant to the facts. Considering the issues I had uncovered; it appeared the leadership were desperate to cover-up their own wrongdoing. Flagrant disregard from men who should have known better, and their behaviour caused irreparable harm to good people.

Litigation was a lengthy stressful process as the courts move slowly and there were times when I was not able to engage in the process, but it did finally conclude with a mediated settlement. As part of the settlement of my civil claim against the church I was asked at the end to sign a non-disclosure agreement. Attempts at cover up right to the end! I refused because the church was accountable to its membership and there could be no non-disclosure on their part. Church leadership did not want their actions known. The senior pastor resigned shortly after the case was settled and I was told he gave instructions to the deacons of the church to make sure he looked good when leaving because his resignation had nothing to do with me! I was abandoned by the church and must question what part of firing a minister with a mental illness is loving, is Christlike?

MENTAL HEALTH AND INSURANCE BATTLES

At the time of my diagnosis, I was working fulltime. I had previously been self-employed with my own counselling practice and was now carrying a reduced caseload in my private practice and working part time as a credentialed minister on the staff of a church, counselling and running several support groups.

Disclosing an experience of mental illness may be beneficial in the workplace to develop strategies designed to aid in continuing employment and guiding coworkers in greater understanding of the difficulties they've noticed but in my situation the disclosure, rather than leading to accommodations to help me, made life more difficult and eventually impossible. As I discovered, discrimination happens, even in a church!

If you are still working or need to take stress leave because of an illness it is vital to research the laws where you live and work before disclosing anything. This is something

I did not do, assuming, because I worked for a church, I didn't need to be concerned. How wrong I was. Most church leadership doesn't know what to do with mental illness, my church leadership couldn't even manage a prayer!

It's my understanding that under Canadian law, employees are not required to disclose the cause of their disability to their employers. You do need to say you're experiencing health challenges, and you must describe what you need to fulfill the responsibilities of your work. ("Mental Illnesses in the Workplace - CMHA National") Your employer may need information from your health care provider around your abilities and difficulties, but they don't need your diagnosis. By law, workplaces must try to make reasonable accommodations for anyone who experiences a disability, including a mental illness. Evidently one in five Canadians will experience a mental illness at some point in their life and many seek disability payments when they are not able to work, but the process of getting to the point of receiving payments is difficult and complicated. Mental illness is often misunderstood by employers resulting in workers having trouble getting the financial aid they need through insurance they have paid for. It is even more of a challenge because many employers and insurance company personnel don't recognize or understand mental illness in the same way as physical illnesses. Providing sufficient medical documentation for long term disability claims and continued eligibility due to mental illness is challenging. Unlike a broken bone, mental illness isn't seen in the same way as an organic cause, like physical brain trauma.

Living with a long-term disability claim due to mental illness was a constant cause of anxiety. I was always wondering "Are they going to stop my payments? Are they going to be happy with what my doctor tells them? Has my psychiatrist given them all the information they need? Are they watching me with a camera, ready to record me doing something I shouldn't be doing on disability". It's a terrible position to be in and all this whilst living with an illness exacerbated by stress!

Lack of awareness about mental health and disability results in more trauma for those battling mental illness. Education is important and necessary for insurers and workplaces, as is the acknowledgement and recognition of mental illnesses as bona fide diseases. I have a file full of documents relating to issues with the company from whom I purchased my insurance that would fill another book if I were to explain them all, but some examples will suffice.

As a self-employed single parent of three, I paid for disability insurance monthly because my children relied on me and my income. Never in my wildest dreams did I expect to use it, but life has a way of presenting us with the unexpected. When I was not able to work because of the illness, every aspect of my life was thrown into disarray, and I made a claim. The company required a second opinion from an out-of-town psychiatrist, a reasonable request. This psychiatrist confirmed the diagnoses, and his conclusion was "the patient is unable to perform the substantial duties of her regular occupation or employment. At the present time, the patient in my opinion is totally disabled."

I was required by the insurance company to keep appointments with my family physician every month, attend appointments with my psychiatrist as recommended and take the medications prescribed. At regular intervals we all had paperwork to complete. This was stressful because I knew the one goal of the insurance company was to deny me benefits as soon as possible. The paperwork was scrutinized for any hint of a reason to deny benefits. I have a copy of a fax my family physician sent to the company at one point when their demands and arguments had escalated beyond all reason. "Please be advised that continual harassment of this lady with respect to her legitimate insurance claim will only exacerbate her delicate mental health problems which have been well documented to you. Further independent exams are spurious, uncalled for and harmful. If you have questions re the legitimacy of her problems, please contact her psychiatrist"

The tax year end for my counselling business was the end of February meaning income earned prior to receiving disability was reported on my income tax return two years after it was earned. The insurance company always wanted copies of my tax returns to make sure I was not earning income, in other words "able to work". As soon as they saw income reported on my tax return half my benefit checks were stopped even though I had highlighted the year of the earnings shown as prior to receiving income from my insurance and included an explanation of the income reported. I tried without success to communicate with the company, they refused to listen. Eventually I was forced to hire a lawyer at my expense to put right the error they had made. I understand the need for checks and balances, but this was going too far, and I felt truly victimized and traumatized by the company for the first time, but it didn't end there.

The next attempt to deny me benefits was in the form of an appointment with a psychiatrist in Vancouver. Apart from struggling with everyday tasks looking after myself I was now expected to attend an appointment with this doctor in Vancouver. My stress soared as they sought a loophole to deny benefits. I phoned the doctor's office requesting a copy of his resume, I may have had bipolar, but I didn't lose my ability to reason. Knowing psychiatrists have different specialties, I wanted to understand his experience with bipolar treatment since his decisions would affect my future. The next thing I heard from the company was a letter telling me the appointment had been cancelled! I wonder why?

Some months went by, but the company was relentless and made an appointment with another psychiatrist. Again, I asked for a resume and informed the doctor's office of my conditions, I would be bringing a witness and tape recording the appointment. This precipitated a phone call from the insurance company, but I stood my ground. Realising I was not going to change my position the representative asked for a copy of the tape, and I agreed. Eventually this appointment was also cancelled. These doctors are hired by companies to decide if a person can return to work. The company is looking for back to work recommendations and I'm sure the doctors who get the most business from the companies are the ones who usually recommend back to work. If the entire system was legitimate, there was surely no problem with the transparency I was demanding. I was fortunate to have the ability to challenge the system but what about those who are not able to? Many are victimized by a broken system. There were no more appointments made for me; I was rightly left in peace to make the best of my situation.

Assessing our mental health is not as simple as measuring our physical health. There are no scales, lab tests or endurance tests to assess mental fitness. A person may answer screening questions in any way they choose but who would want to buy and consume high doses of antidepressants and mood stabilising drugs if they didn't need them to function, who would choose a life with bipolar? How many psychiatrists prescribe drugs for someone who doesn't need them? There may be exceptions, but should society focus on the possible exceptions rather than looking at the picture created over time by a persons' psychiatrist? Society and insurance personnel need to change the way it views mental illness and how individuals are treated.

Travelling On

Oh, the torment of the past
That rages in my soul,
Unleashed by the promise of wholeness
Which seems so elusive and unreal.
Will the dark night ever end?
Will peaceful sleep engage me ever again?
Or will I stagger through the desert
From one mirage to the next?
Longing for a connection with
        Something,
                someone?
No, the die is cast
And true to form relentlessly I'll tread
Walking out each day and night
With everything I dread.

The hope was there
But slowly fades
As step by step I go
A lonely traveller
On this never-ending road.
Too distant
    Far away
        I'm lost
Out of reach to this poor traveller.

SUPPORTING INDIVIDUALS WITH MENTAL ILLNESS

You may have a connection to someone with a mental illness through your living situation, family relationships, colleagues, friends, associates or neighbors; all different relationships involving various levels and amounts of contact but all potentially valuable and therefore important. Living with a mental illness is difficult and sometimes exhausting as is having a relationship with a person struggling with mental illness. You cannot rescue them, but you can offer support. The symptoms of mental illness can be painful or embarrassing and it is difficult not to take them personally, but these behaviours are not selfish or immature.

Research confirms the importance of this support from family, friends and associates as a key part of helping a person who is going through a mental illness, providing a network of practical and emotional help. However, these relationships can require a lot of effort at times.

Dealing with the ups and downs of bipolar disorder, distortions in thinking and behavior, the late-night phone calls, and the nagging fear of a potential suicide attempt is not easy. Living with an individual who has bipolar disorder can cause stress and tension and family members often struggle with their own feelings of guilt, fear, anger, and helplessness. In any relationship it is important to balance supporting others with self-care. Be aware of your boundaries and understand professional help is sometimes necessary, as family and friends may not be able to provide the same level of support. Individuals with a mental illness may need to be encouraged to seek help, keep appointments and maintain the prescribed medication regimen.

Expectations of us can be terrifying because we are not being difficult, we never know when we will be up or down. Mental illness doesn't make much sense to those whose brains function in the more usual way but when you don't understand don't condemn. At least be willing to accept the struggles without judgement and without trying to make it logical for you. I'm amazed at the explanations created by others for my behaviour in order to make it fit with their beliefs. Utter fabrications bearing no resemblance to truth but "they have it all figured out".

Depression and mania can cause one's perception of the world to change dramatically. This can be both exhausting and frustrating. Mania can be a great feeling but doesn't always last and the lack of predictability is difficult for all concerned. Bipolar disorder is a unique experience, and most cannot imagine what it's like to experience mania. On one hand, they may falsely romanticize it and expect it to be wonderful to have seemingly endless energy; on the other hand, falsely scandalizing it and expecting someone with mania to be dangerous or violent. Neither of these reflect what it's like to have this condition. It is probably easier to relate to depression or anxiety than bipolar disorder. Although we usually explain mood swings in terms of highs and lows, individuals with bipolar don't experience all happy feelings when in a state of mania. Everyone feels highs and lows, but individuals with bipolar disorder are experiencing those extremes much more, and it's hard to understand what it must be like. Individuals often feel incredibly empowered; however, every episode of mania comes with a deep slide into depression. The highs of mania take incredible amounts of energy, it's exhausting. It's important to balance expectations.

Whether it's a period of mania, or weeks in the depths of depression, stability and love are critical. Individuals with a mental illness often feel isolated, spending even short periods of time with them helps. Suggest going for coffee or taking a walk together which provides a change of space and some company. Bipolar disorder comes with a lot of unusual experiences, but deep down each one longs to live a "normal" life as much as possible, we want to be treated like everybody else.

Bipolar can be stabilized with proper treatment, medication, and the patience, love, and understanding of friends and family. Medications do not affect everyone equally. As a result, each individual may have to work through different medications to find the best balance. Talking about the issue with someone we trust will often provide the insight and understanding we are searching for and enable us to move forward.

The life of an individual with bipolar disorder is filled with extremes. Those highly productive times are exhilarating, but it is important to recognize that this is not a healthy way to live. Between episodes the temptation to stop the medication and get some colour back into life is sometimes overwhelming.

As a support, learning as much as you can about mental illness, treatment and what services are available in your area will be helpful to gain an understanding of how the symptoms may come and go and vary in severity and how you can help. It is important to decide what level of relationship you are realistically willing to have without feeling overwhelmed and resentful. Be clear about those boundaries, honest, kind and consistent in your relationship. Take care of yourself both emotionally and physically to cope better with the stress of a relationship with your friend or family member. Allowing yourself to be depleted by being with others is never helpful and can have disastrous consequences. Having caring, supportive friends and family to confide in is vital but often people want to help, get too involved and then run leaving a person confused and hurting.

Those suffering emotional turmoil are often self-conscious and fearful of being seen as 'not normal.' The self-consciousness can lead to feeling too stigmatized to seek help or to be honest about their feelings. It is incredibly hurtful when a person, intentionally or by accident, uses phrases perpetuating a view of mental illness as shameful or tiresome rather than something suffered by many more than we realize. Everyone has a right to their own feelings. They may not be rational but are real and therefore matter. Answer questions truthfully, avoid debates and intense conversations.

Telling individuals with a mental illness to "get over it," or "it's not really that bad" is hurtful. We wouldn't dream of saying to a person with his or her leg in a cast, "You don't need a cast. Take it off and put your foot down like everyone else!" Why do many find it acceptable to say a person with an anxiety disorder, "Just don't worry about it"? Eliminating words such as "crazy" or "insane" is a small but vital way to reduce the stigma attached to such language. These put-downs make light of what someone feels and can give the impression they think a choice is being made about these difficult emotions. Anyone with an anxiety disorder knows they worry a lot. Telling us to do things we're not able to do adds to our feelings of failure and inadequacy. Friends and family may get frustrated and make hurtful and unhelpful comments like "Snap out of it!", "What is wrong?", "Aren't you over that yet?" or "Didn't those pills work?" when what we need is support and acceptance. Much better to say, "This must be hard for you," or "I'm here if you want to talk about how you feel." Focus on showing empathy and a willingness to listen which will avoid adding to out of control emotions. Let them lead the discussion. Talking requires trust and courage. You might be the first contact they have been able to talk to about this. You may not be a medical expert or a trained counsellor, but you can still offer support. You can say "Would you like to tell me how you are feeling?" Try to keep your language neutral. Paraphrase back what is said to you to confirm you have understood correctly. Show you respect their feelings. Don't take control, decisions are not yours to make! "How can I make it feel safe for you?" "Can you help me understand that?", "How can I help?" Affirm the persons value and purpose. Celebrate successes, however small and short lived. It is best to listen and try to understand as much as possible. Peer support and self-help groups are invaluable in this regard, providing a safe and non-judgemental place for social interaction. Support groups provide access to others with shared experiences, a sense of belonging, role models and encouragement.

Knowing what to say is sometimes challenging but these are some of the messages we need to hear, reminders we need often:

> "You are not the illness."
> "Bipolar disorder is a real illness, like diabetes. It requires medical treatment."
> "You're not to blame. You didn't cause this. It's not your fault."
> "You can feel better. There are many treatments that can help."
> "Avoiding treatment isn't helpful."

It is difficult when someone you care about is not willing to acknowledge the possibility of a mental illness. Perhaps suggest a routine medical checkup instead, or a doctor's visit for a specific symptom, such as insomnia, irritability, or fatigue (you can privately call ahead to tell the doctor of your concerns about bipolar disorder). Not all medical professionals understand all mental illnesses and how to treat them. Help your friend or family member find a professional who has good understanding of their particular illness.

It is important to be aware, to pick up when a depressed individual isn't coping, to notice when routine tasks are neglected and pitch in to help. These are some examples of what helped for me. Don't assume this is the same for everyone. Find out what your friend, partner, neighbor, parent needs. Proper food and sleep are important, and one friend would often phone me around supper time to ask what I was planning to eat, many times the response was "I haven't decided!" The conversation would end with an invitation for supper at five and I was expected! I was invited to lead a bible study at a church I was attending but declined, explaining there were days I couldn't function. The response was that the person would be happy to fill in for me if I couldn't be there. I didn't pursue the opportunity, but it was encouraging to know I was welcome, my situation was understood and accepted, and support was there for me if I needed it. When I first joined a church choir, there were some stressful times but two of the choir members were particularly sensitive to my needs and supported me through those situations.

During one of the difficult periods with the illness I struggled to decide what to wear and getting up and dressed every day was a challenge. One of my daughters put together cards with complete outfits written out. I could pick up a card, get dressed and know at least I looked OK!

One year when I laid on the bed all summer with my dog, a friend came over regularly and kept my garden under control until I was feeling better and able to do it again.

Sometimes I needed to connect with the reality of another human being and there was usually someone I could connect with. When I was depressed and having difficulty completing necessary tasks a friend would help by asking what needed to be done, figuring out the time needed and planning to connect when the task was done. This was helpful and often it only took ten or fifteen minutes, but it was done!

Other friends would go shopping with me which made it much easier because shopping would sometimes generate an excess of anxiety.

During my time of ministry, I kept all the "thank you" notes I received and during the darkest times I would get them out to encourage myself by reading them, realising my life did have purpose and meaning, thank you to all those who wrote those notes. There were those who turned away when I needed help but many more who stepped up to be there for me.

I cannot complete this chapter without the story of a friend who stoically stood her ground for me when I was in a stressful situation. A group I knew were travelling from Canada to an event in the United States and wanted me to come. The travel involved several changes of transportation which I knew were more than I could cope with, and I reluctantly declined. One of the group assured me she would stay close to ensure my safety. It was tempting, and I finally agreed. The outgoing travel and the event went without any problem, and I had a positive experience but coming home we were separated in the customs hall at Toronto airport, and I panicked! There was not much time to make the next connection, and it involved travelling to a different terminal. I managed to find my way to the bus which was not leaving in time to catch my connection. My stress level was going up and the bus driver would not leave until he had more passengers, I was stuck and the departure time for my next flight was far too close for comfort but there was no help from the bus driver. We finally left the terminal, and I knew I would not arrive at the new departure gate in time but, maybe the flight would be delayed for some reason. As soon as I got off the bus, I found someone with a golf cart and quickly told my situation. I jumped on and we took off at great speed. As we came flying round the corner to the gate, I saw my friend engaged in animated conversation. She told the gate agents that her friend had health issues, and she refused to leave until I arrived. She explained the flight could either wait or they could remove her luggage and she would take a later flight with me. She chose not to take the easy route and leave me behind, I was grateful. Sometimes helping others means making difficult, challenging choices, and staying true to commitments made.

It's helpful when people can communicate their needs but those with a mental illness may not always be able to.

Making it safe for a person to ask for help is important but understand when it doesn't happen and watch for indications help is needed.

An individual struggling with mental illness can be in a dark place at times. If you sense a person is at serious risk of suicide, stay with them if possible and contact the psychiatric emergency team at your local hospital. Or call your local emergency number and explain that they are suicidal, have made a plan, and you have concerns for their safety. Know what to do in a crisis, who to call.

Sadly, friends and family do not always know how to respond to us. Our depression and manic behavior are sometimes too much, and they avoid us, not knowing how to help. We also isolate ourselves, then the adage "Out of sight, out of mind" fits and people move on.

In my experience many cannot relate to the unending battle of this illness or understand the frustration of knowing what little relief there is often doesn't last. Hurt feelings can heal over time if relationships do fall apart and distorted views about mental illness can be corrected if there is some motivation. Yes, some relationships are toxic and must be avoided. With motivation, people can surprise you by changing their thinking and restoring relationships. Many do not understand how severely mental illness can affect our lives, some will learn, others will not. The widespread misconceptions make it difficult to talk to friends and family and more education and understanding would be helpful. What do we need? We need you to be with us in this moment, be present in the now. Don't expect us to be like we were yesterday, whether we were in a good space or not we may not be the same today. Offer grace even when not able to relate, it is not necessary to totally understand something to be understanding. Don't pressure us to be in the place you want us to be, be with us where we are now.

When?

How the anguish of the night churns in my soul
What might have been
Time remains
How long, how far
Till journeys end?

Morning light breaks through my thoughts
I journey on another day
How will this day be
Today till night falls once again?

I can rise up and be all that I was made to be in this day
Not yesterday or tomorrow but
today dawning bright for me and all that I am.

Will I embrace the dawn
Breathe the fresh air for this day
Or will I crawl away
Disappointed once again
as the sun sets
on another opportunity
lost for eternity?

SPACES FOR EMOTIONAL WELL BEING

Imagine walking into a room where you feel completely at ease, where your thoughts and feelings are valued, and where you can express yourself without fear of judgment. This is the essence of a safe space, a sanctuary for mental health and emotional well-being. In today's world, the need for these spaces has never been greater. Whether within our families, among friends, or in our places of worship, creating environments that foster safety and support is crucial for our collective well-being.

Life has taught me to be aware of creating safe spaces wherever we are and whoever we are with, and I believe there is room for greater awareness of this in every area of our lives. I have drawn on my own experience in family, various group situations and churches where deficiencies were highlighted as a result of mental illness, but we all need to experience safe places. None of us can ever really know what the person next to us is going through, none of us know what past pain may be triggered by a thoughtless comment and I have been guilty on more than one occasion of making those comments. However, we can try to take more time to think before we speak and act to make sure our impact on a conversation is supportive, helpful and encouraging.

Mental illness is no respecter of persons, class, or family background. For me, the abuse in my home contributed to my illness and resulted in my inability to cope with life in a healthy way. Each family member needs to know they are loved and accepted for who they are, not what they can do or contribute. Mistakes and failures are part of life and expected, accepted and surrounded with support in a healthy family. During the inevitable times of disappointment and challenges a healthy family will provide a safety net enabling a person to move through the situation and emerge psychologically unscathed. As a family builds positive relationships by solving problems together, celebrating each other's successes and showing empathy to one another, each member can experience emotional safety. This process can build internal resilience to life's difficulties. A supportive family environment strengthens relationships and helps prevent mental health issues such as anxiety and depression. Families that maintain healthy dynamics spend time together and share common values and interests. Good mental health does not mean feeling good all the time, but it does mean being able to cope with stress and life changes whilst keeping good relationships. On the other hand, a toxic family dynamic may involve one or more members treating each other in harmful or destructive ways when faced with challenges and struggles. In these situations, angry outbursts, violation of boundaries, lying, blame, manipulation, control and verbal, emotional, or physical abuse will be on display. Frequently, neglect, abuse, addiction, secrecy and denial are the products of these families. Chaos, uncertainty and exhaustion replace safety.

Poor communication is a frequent cause of family conflict. Not feeling heard or being overlooked can lead to hurt and frustration expressed as anger. It's important to create opportunity for family members to communicate in a relaxed environment and mealtimes can provide occasion for round the table family discussions, even once or twice a week set aside for a family meal would enable some healthy discussion. A family activity also provides opportunity for healthy interaction. These days, most families no longer wash dishes together, a time that once fostered sharing family stories and enjoyable conversation.

Healthy, safe communication can be learned, and family is the earliest opportunity for this to happen. It is important to focus on listening and understanding what the other person is trying to say and not interrupting while they are speaking; actively listening to what they are saying and what they mean; checking your understanding by asking questions or paraphrasing what they've said and expressing your side of the story clearly and honestly to promote positive communication. Showing interest by asking questions and listening to the ideas of others; talking and listening to feelings and experiences; reassuring others you care about them by voice tone and body language as well as the words spoken and avoiding sarcastic remarks and comments demeaning others or causing embarrassment will encourage everyone's participation. It's perfectly acceptable to talk about feelings and if you do lose your temper, talk about what happened, why you are angry and apologize if you were wrong!

Providing family structure and boundaries will promote a safe environment in the home. A team of landscape architects conducted a simple study to observe any physical and psychological influences of having fences around playgrounds and how its effects would impact preschool children. On playgrounds without fences the children tended to gather around the teacher and were reluctant to stray far from her view. On fenced playgrounds they ran around the entire playground feeling more free to explore. ("Fenced-in playgrounds: how boundaries can encourage greater creativity"). Rather than being a limiting factor, boundaries create safe situations to explore. I believe this applies to relationships in families where expectations and norms provide boundaries for safe interactions.

Healthy, happy families have parents leading by example, open communication, clear expectations and limits and process for conflict management. They foster independence of each family member by accommodating differences, encouraging and praising positive behaviors and choices. Healthy families stick together, have fun and laugh together.

A safe space is a supportive non-threatening environment where all the participants in a group are comfortable to express themselves and share experiences without fear of discrimination or reprisal. A group in this context applies to any gathering, family, friends, associates or specific group activities such as study groups, therapy or support groups. The group may be social time after work, a coffee morning gathering, work group meeting or any one of a multitude of occasions. Creating a safe space is especially important when dealing with mental health issues but we all need to feel safe in group situations. Unfortunately, there are too many settings where little or no attention is paid to emotional safety. In these days of communication by text we have set aside some of the words used in the past to add respect and consideration to our conversation such as "please", "thank you", "you're welcome", "pardon me", "excuse me",

"I'm sorry". The demise of basic "good manners" has resulted in an attitude of "it doesn't matter" contributing to escalating stress and anxiety in group situations.

It does matter, the wellbeing of people other than ourselves does matter and we can make a difference by the way we conduct ourselves. Safe conversation acknowledges all the participants by introductions and makes them at ease by being friendly, listening, and showing interest. We can respect physical and emotional boundaries; respect the identity and backgrounds of others; not assume or make judgments about a person's gender identity, sexual preference, survivor status, health status, economic status, religious background, beliefs or opinions. Respectful communication will mean not pushing anyone to answer questions they don't want to answer and not to share anyone else's personal stories without their permission. Yes, there may be times when our words or actions have an effect we didn't intend but a person's feelings are valid regardless of our intentions. It is helpful to assume positive intent if someone does or says something upsetting for you and appropriate to gently let them know how you feel.

A safe conversation means you are being spoken with, not at; life experience is validated not labeled as wrong because it's different; there is no criticism or judgment; it puts participants at ease and doesn't offend. Don't interrupt in a group but take your turn to speak and avoid monopolising the conversation, be careful to include everyone in the group. Inside jokes and asides are not acceptable. We can all make a difference and improve the experience for all in group situations with a little extra thought and consideration.

Most churches are as helpless in the face of mental illness as the rest of the population. They frequently have little to offer and feel impotent when they meet mental illness face to face. In my case church leadership behaved as though they thought they could do what they liked with me and get away with it, so much for church "fellowship". Their response reflected attitudes and actions of the dark ages focused on "getting rid" of a person with a mental illness. Organizations have an important responsibility to support individuals and communities as they navigate their lives, and this principle should be upheld in all institutions.

Christians who have been abused will often choose either to seek help outside the church or learn to handle the damage by pretending it does not exist. There is a need in our churches to think long and hard about tough problems like abuse and then make appropriate changes. The damage done to me through abuse was heinous, it distorted my relationship with God and robbed me of childhoods' carefree, trusting relationships. Through no fault of my own I was subjected to terrible crimes against my own soul that set in motion behaviours reflecting my pain.

Mental illness is as real as any other physical illness, we are comfortable helping someone who needs assistance because of a physical ailment but brush off depression as "just having a rough time". Everyone knows something is wrong but mostly we don't talk about it. As a church we need to acknowledge and accept that mental illness is a real thing, making life difficult for those who suffer with it. Possibilities are then opened up for victims to share their struggles and for the church community to support and encourage. For genuine interactions to occur there must be reality and acceptance. There needs to be help for the body, mind and the soul together, the physical and the spiritual, as both are engaged in the struggle.

With depression there are real, physical symptoms, feelings of hopelessness or overwhelming sadness, or total exhaustion for no apparent reason. Honest, helpful, care means coming alongside by encouraging, helping to find appropriate medical treatment and praying. Telling a mentally ill person to "just stop" makes things worse for them. It's alright to not understand mental illness but it's not helpful to give advice, believe it is what it is and trust what the person says. By all means pray but don't try to fix it! It's not helpful to tell a person with a mental illness to try harder, pray harder, believe harder, or work harder. They can't! What we do need is practical help when we're unable to do for ourselves.

Churches can promote a sense of belonging for those with a mental illness through welcoming hospitality. This involves thinking more positively about mental illness and fostering positive attitudes and behaviors. Engaging individuals with mental illness requires strength to identify with their suffering, the courage to befriend them, and the ability to recognize their courage. The church has a responsibility to be a voice for the voiceless by advocating for them and educating others about their conditions. People struggling with mental health challenges should have opportunities to participate in whatever way they are able in church life.

Pastors can encourage emotional safety in their churches by equipping church leaders with knowledge about trauma and its effects and how to recognize a person in distress. It's okay not to have all the answers, walk alongside the hurting giving them a space to safely share their struggles and receive support without shame and free from the fear of negative comments and gossip. Yes, it is hard to understand but if you are finding it hard to understand it might help to pause and consider how hard mental illness might be to live with.

For a church congregation to be supportive without enabling harmful behaviors there needs to be opportunity for education in the form of relevant workshops and seminars to empower and encourage family members and friends of those dealing with mental health issues. Admitting to a need for help takes courage and is not a sign of weakness. However, when experiencing a mental health problem, it may be easier to speak to friends and family before a health professional, so knowing how to support and encourage appropriate connections is helpful. Learning how to listen can be taught and learned to improve the quality of any interaction.

Churches can take the lead in breaking the silence and stigma around mental health by encouraging open dialogue about emotional struggles, creating a safe place where individuals are accepted, understood and valued. Allow the sharing of personal stories and mental health journeys without criticism, judgement or glib solutions. Christians are called to pray and weep alongside each other. A safe church will have resources for those who struggle, bible studies, recovery groups, counseling, prayer ministries. However, unless the leadership are on board, programs will not guarantee a safe place for someone with a mental illness as I experienced. If the church in my situation had acted appropriately my losses would not have been as great as they were.

Creating safe spaces is a necessity for fostering mental health and emotional well-being in our families, groups, and churches. As we navigate the complexities of modern life, it is crucial to remember that our words and actions have the power to uplift or harm those around us. By being mindful of our interactions and striving to create environments where everyone feels valued and supported, we can make a significant difference in the lives of others.

I encourage you to take the lessons from this chapter to heart and put them into practice. Evaluate the spaces you inhabit, your home, your social circles, and your places of worship. Are these spaces truly safe for everyone? Are there ways to improve communication, set healthier boundaries, and offer more support? Consider these steps to create and maintain safe places.

In your family: Foster open communication, show empathy, and celebrate each other's successes. Create opportunities for relaxed discussions and ensure that everyone feels heard and valued.

In your groups: Promote respectful communication, avoid judgment, and include everyone in conversations. Be mindful of the impact of your words and actions on others.

In your church: Advocate for mental health awareness, provide support for those struggling, and create a welcoming environment. Encourage open dialogue and offer resources for those in need.

Creating safe spaces is an ongoing process that requires commitment and effort. By making a conscious effort to support and uplift those around us, we can build a more compassionate and understanding world; we can work together to create safe spaces where everyone can thrive.

Theodore Roosevelt
"This country will not be a good place to live in
unless we make it a good place for all of us to live in".
("TR Center - This Country will not...be a good place...")

EMERGING FROM THE SHADOWS

I was diagnosed with bipolar in 1993 and had a severe episode in 1995 bringing along with it significant cognitive impairment and ending my working life. It became evident I had lived with bipolar for most of my life and I was now taking the highest recommended dose of antidepressants plus mood stabilizer drugs to keep me functioning.

This episode closed the door on life as I had known it, I was a prisoner in the jail of the illness. My life had been ripped away. I lost job, ministry, family and friends, trapped without hope in a life I had not chosen, a life inflicted on me. I was living in the same body but now with a distorted mind not able to function adequately. Emotions, I was unable to understand or control, were running rampant through my life. The illness, initially no big deal, had now become my prison.

Following my horrendous experiences of church life and bipolar I lost many positive aspects of my Christian life. Much of my thinking and belief was distorted or destroyed.

No longer reading my bible, no church home, and my Christian social connections were shattered. I was cut loose from what had always been a strong anchor for me and I was in no state mentally or emotionally to do much about it. I tried to attend other evangelical churches but everything I heard, and saw was coloured by my earlier negative experience, and nothing offered a way forward.

Through one of my many failed businesses attempts I met someone who has become a dear friend. In her I saw something I wanted for myself and although I couldn't define the "something", I determined to find out what it was. Our friendship grew and we shared openly about our different perspectives on spirituality. After a while, the reason for our connection became clear when she gave me a book called "Open Your Mind to Receive" by Catherine Ponder, a Unity Church minister based in the United States. Initially reluctant, I did eventually read it and was introduced to the principles of the Law of Attraction. I studied, attended workshops and read books by Bob Proctor, Michael Losier, Earl Nightingale, Rhonda Byrne, James Allen, Robin Sharma, Napoleon Hill and Raymond Holliwell. The focus of all this material maintained that it is possible to attract riches into our lives and as my life at the time felt depleted in every way, I was open to any path with the possibility of leading to some abundance. It did not result in thousands of dollars in my bank account or fancy cars, but I learned how the words I speak, and my thoughts have consequences, they trigger responses, and I have the power to choose what I say and what I think thus determining the outcome. I decided to start consciously choosing, to make changes, remove negatives from my life; negative thoughts, negative people, negative words, negative television, negative reading, negative actions and my friend was persistent in keeping me accountable and calling me out when I fell back into negative talk! With greater understanding and insight, I continued the process until the negative thought patterns were removed. This made a lot of sense and was all remarkably interesting, but I knew my life was still not going in the right direction and the bipolar illness continued to wreak its havoc. My life felt like an empty shell struggling through each day, emotionally stabilized by a collection of medications. I can't even begin to itemise everything I did to try and change my situation, to do better, to create an income for myself, to beat the illness, get on top of it, always hopeful the next idea would be the answer and change my situation, but it didn't, and the illness continued to progress unhindered by my efforts. Throughout this period, only a few close friends were aware of the circumstances in my life, as I mostly kept it private.

Ignorance about mental health seems to be behind the behaviour of many individuals. Few were interested in having a conversation with me about my journey, to listen with understanding. It's a lonely walk and the hell of mental illness is endured for the most part alone.

One Sunday morning I turned on the television and came across a Christian program. I was drawn into what was spoken, lights went on for me and hope started to rise as I listened to the teaching. The ministry distributes a free magazine, I immediately ordered it, and the front cover of the first copy I received had the headline "Get on the Right Road". I still have the copy with all my underlining. I typed up significant portions of the article and repeatedly read them aloud as affirmations. I connected to the website online and began watching all the video teachings. The teaching was making sense to me and answering questions I had never been able to find answers to before, the dots were starting to connect, the puzzle pieces began to form a picture. As I studied, I became more aware of the sad life I was trying to live and began to consider the possibility of healing. The idea was ridiculous! Everything I read and all I was told about bipolar was that it can be managed but not healed.

The teaching that thoughts and words have consequences made sense to me and if I said I was depressed I would be, if I said I couldn't cope I wouldn't be able to. The image for me was simple "if I told my arm to lift up then it did, if I told it to bang on the table then it did." If my arm responded to the commands of my brain, then so should the other parts of my being. I needed to tell my mind and body what I wanted it to do and be!

I learned all about positive confessions, searched for ones that fit my situation, mostly bible verses, and fed on them regularly throughout my day as I paced the floor in my condominium. I read them aloud to hear them, I took them like medication to build my faith and heal my sick body and mind. I was not willing to limp along anymore. God was either all God or not God at all, and if He was all God then maybe healing was possible.

One of the speakers I listened to online was an American pastor living with his family in Russia, pastoring a Christian church of thousands in Moscow and I regularly tuned in to the daily bible study. On one of these programs, he introduced Dr. Caroline Leaf, a cognitive neuroscientist and committed Christian who explained "Science and spirituality are compatible. The Bible tells the story, and science explains how the Bible and scriptures play out." Science is not in conflict with God at all. Science simply explains to us the intricacies of creation, how it's all put together and how it works.

Dr. Caroline Leaf studied how the brain can change with directed mind input and has transformed the lives of hundreds of thousands of individuals with traumatic brain injury, learning disabilities, ADHD, autism, dementia and mental ill-health issues like anxiety and depression. Dr. Leaf teaches the science behind how to recognize negative patterns and turn destructive thoughts into healthy thoughts. Whether you are a person of science, a person of faith, or somewhere in between this teaching is life changing.

It is now recognised from research and experience how the mind can change the brain. We all have a mess in our brains. How we manage the mess is the difference between a healthy mind and body and a mind and body riddled with anxiety and depression. Putting this teaching into practice has significantly impacted my mental health and I guard my mind with great care now. I carefully manage my life to avoid negative talk and behaviour.

As I continued to research this material, I was increasingly drawn to study my bible once again and found the underlying principles of the Law of Attraction and how the brain functions are not in conflict. Dr. Leaf's teaching made everything clear to me, and I am grateful.

My belief in church fellowship motivated me to keep trying, to keep looking for a church home. Since then, I've attended several churches of different denominations but haven't regained what I lost. I'm hesitant, lack trust, and don't feel completely safe in church communities. I tried attending evangelical churches but there were too many triggers for the pain not yet fully healed. I finally found myself in a United Church, surprised because their theology was different from mine, but I found peace and healing there; the church welcomed me, loved me and provided a safe place at that time for me to heal. No one was pushing and no one was judging.

We may want to choose how, when and if we will be healed but those decisions aren't ours to make. There are frequently issues other than physical healing God is working out in our lives. I needed to make changes in my life to be as healthy and productive as possible and I made those changes as I was able.

I don't know what your pathway looks like, I am only able to recount what happened to me as I understand it. I sought after the real God. I had heard enough about a god who might answer prayer or might not; a god who sometimes cared and other times turned a blind eye; a god who allows sickness, pain and suffering to teach his children how to behave. I was not able to reconcile this god with the Christ I know and have experienced.

I continued to focus on my relationship with God and enjoy a more positive life and then I became aware of some different feelings. I puzzled over it, wondering what was happening, I wasn't depressed and then I wondered if I was over medicated, it was a mystery! I hadn't experienced this before, what was it? A few days passed before I started to wonder if God had actually healed me and was I now over-medicated? How do I go to my psychiatrist, and tell her I've been healed? Maybe I need to take it in stages? Where do I start? I asked if it would be possible to cut back on my anti-depressants as I had been feeling much better. My medications were reduced a little with an admonishment making it clear this was only the antidepressants; the mood stabilisers were not going to be changed. I was of retirement age by this time, no longer receiving disability insurance payments, no longer subject to the requirements of the insurance company. The process of ending my dependence on medication had started, I agreed to reducing the antidepressants and doing it according to the timetable set by my psychiatrist.

I left the appointment excited to discover what would happen. At my next appointment, having not experienced any depression, I did tell my psychiatrist how I believed I had been healed and received a respectful response. I committed to whatever she thought was best in terms of timing the reduction of my medication. Over the next year the dosage of antidepressants was gradually reduced until I was free of medication for depression. What next? My psychiatrist had made it clear she would not make any changes to the mood stabilising medication but if, as I genuinely believed, I was healed then I didn't need them. During my next appointment I carefully broached the issue of the mood stabilising drugs wondering if it was possible to try reducing the dose! My psychiatrist went into deep thought and then responded, "Why not, we have nothing to lose?". We reviewed what to do if something went wrong, but I was confident all would be well, and it was. A year later I took my last dose of medication and have been completely symptom and medication free ever since. The cognitive impairments were also healed although old habit patterns do try to come back sometimes, and I need to keep a tight rein on my thought life!

There were many sources shaping my healing journey and I believe they all played a part. The principles of the Law of Attraction taught me the power of positive thinking and the impact of words and thoughts on my life. Dr. Caroline Leaf's teachings on neuroplasticity and the compatibility of science and spirituality significantly affected my mental health. Similarly Cognitive Behavior Therapy (CBT) focuses on the connection between thoughts, emotions and behaviors. Unhelpful or distorted thinking patterns can lead to emotional distress and problematic behaviors but all these patterns can be identified and changed. In CBT practical skills are learned to reframe negative thoughts, regulate emotions, and develop more healthy coping strategies. Despite negative experiences with church life, I have found churches, which provide a safe space for me to heal and grow. My healing journey involved making conscious choices to believe that healing was possible through faith and the right environment for the brain to heal itself.

I am writing my story to give hope to others that there are ways to live a better life with bipolar disorder. Whether it was a supernatural intervention or a combination of factors, what has happened to me is thrilling. I got my life back and want it to be a possibility for all.

The Door

There is a door that I must walk through
A door which is hiding, far away in the mist.
As the sunshine of the day breaks through,
the door becomes more clear

Briefly, it seems, as a moment in time
I can see clearly only to watch the mist of evening cloud
the vision I had.

What a bittersweet conflict
as the vision of my door declines to show itself clearly.

I reach out, to move toward the door
doubting the confidence I need to move ahead
A hand touches mine and my step is secure
I am moving ahead with rhythm to my stride
The door becomes clear
and I embrace the risk of walking through.
No one knows what is on the other side
No one else will walk the road for me
But a hand still touches mine and I continue to move
ahead.
In a moment I arrive and pass through, my heart pound-
ing in its appointed place.

The road continues on the other side, and I stride it out
with joy.

THROUGH THE FOG A PATH EMERGES

Walking out of this illness was as lonely and painful as walking into it. When my healing became a reality, I started talking about it, but the responses overall were far from encouraging. Few were able to rejoice with me: most were sceptical at best. Understandable because wherever you research bipolar you will read the same verdict "there may be periods of time with no symptoms but there is no cure". One or two friends were able to engage with me in a conversation about it but often my attempts were met with silence. Being healed elicited a similar response to having the illness. No one wants to talk about it, they either say nothing or change the subject. It was easy to guess what they might be thinking and some of these thoughts were spoken to me.

> "Let's see how long this lasts, she'll have another episode sooner or later".
> "I knew it – she was never sick, used it when it

> suited her, good excuse if you ask me".
> "I'm keeping quiet, don't want to get involved in this one, doesn't make any sense to me".
> "That's ridiculous, you don't get healed of bipolar".

Individuals are sometimes more comfortable with their own perceptions than truth and reality. "You need to earn your way back into the family" !! I wanted to scream until there was no scream left in me. I wasn't a naughty child who was too badly behaved to be with the rest of the family. Rape had triggered a horrible mental illness, and I was the victim struggling to survive and longing for someone to show they cared, but I kept silent and went on my way with the scream still inside me. I had been robbed of everything that was me and I was replaced by bipolar.

Rather than thinking about my situation, they were dealing with their own issues around the subject of mental illness. Was I healed? If the answer is yes, then there is a reality in this most don't want to consider. Some commented, "it's over now, put it behind you". However, to walk out I had to walk through it all again and grieve the losses and feel the pain with no medication now to dull the feelings to bearable.

The need to grieve the losses associated with mental illness is often overlooked. Mental illness can alter self-perception and identity leading to the feelings of disconnection from one's earlier sense of self. Individuals facing mental health challenges may mourn loss of relationships or strained relationships with family, friends or colleagues resulting from the symptoms or stigma associated with mental health conditions. Opportunities, career aspirations, educational goals or personal ambitions might be disrupted or deferred due to the impact of mental illness.

This form of grief is characterized by the absence of clear closure or understanding. Unlike traditional grief where the loss is definitive and recognized, ambiguous loss leaves individuals in a state of uncertainty that complicates the grieving process.

Allowing time and opportunity to grieve the intangible losses of mental illness can lead to self-forgiveness for the time lost and the hardships endured. The process requires courage and bravery to honor experiences and make space for uncomfortable and difficult emotions. It is a personal journey and there is no right or wrong way to experience it but with time, embracing and processing these feelings can bring a path towards healing and acceptance.

One or two friends lasted through the twenty years, from diagnosis to healing, but mostly they either couldn't cope, or I pushed them away when my illness was acting out. I couldn't do the things others did. I was as crippled mentally and emotional as much as if I'd been in a wheelchair except wheelchairs are visible and understood, mental illness is not. My intelligent mind would not work the way it was created to function, and I found this incredibly frustrating. I had post high school education in three disciplines and couldn't tell the time correctly to get to an appointment. This I never did fully understand.

In the twenty years, since the diagnosis, my place in the family had mostly been replaced. Others had come in as I was squeezed further and further out. My oldest daughter and her first husband had divorced and both married again with the new spouses having families who became additional family to my granddaughters. My ex-husband left his second wife and was now with a partner who had a daughter. My youngest daughter married and settled in the same town as her in-laws, providing her children with other family to take my place. I was included minimally in family occasions and although some presented the pros of not having to do the "family thing" it still hurt. After raising my children as a single parent with no support from my ex-husband other than a financial agreement he challenged regularly, I was left out in the cold like a leper outside the walls of my family.

As I moved back into circulation, I became aware of the shift in family dynamics. I was the mother who appeared out of nowhere, and some didn't know I existed. At one particular social gathering, it became apparent that my ex-husband's partner was thought to be the mother of his children, it cut deep and hurt. This misconception had not been previously corrected and now created an uncomfortable situation for all those present. It was laughed off, the conversation moved on and I was left with a wound that had been ripped open.

I became aware of missing pieces in my life. gaps in the picture like pieces missing from a puzzle. I lost pieces of myself during the traumatic times and the growth of some pieces was stunted and crippled by illness. I lost joy in learning, in new experiences, in setting and achieving goals; I lost relationships, roots in a church, friends, siblings. Some of these pieces were irretrievable, some may be restored, time would tell what my future path would be. I wanted to live my life, to be who I am; to do what I was created to do. I didn't know how to do it, but intended to find out, to search out the truth about who I am and who I was before I was violated and before my identity was twisted and obscured.

I had committed to coming off the medications according to my psychiatrist timetable. I respected all she had done for me over the years, and I thought it was possible to walk away from the medications with no ill effects if I did it right. It was a two-year journey and when I came out the other side, opened my eyes and looked at my life it was a mess. Life did not instantly become OK. The closest analogy in my thinking is of a dry drunk, someone who has given up drinking but still has the habit patterns of an active alcoholic. My focus then was on how to change, how to create a meaningful life.

I had a life again and the opportunity to shape the future, something I doubt many have experienced. The thought was overwhelming at times, exciting, scary, confusing, intimidating. I started by thoughtfully considering what brought me joy and this involved digging deep as I hadn't experienced much joy in the last few years. I was unsure of what I was capable of, of what might be possible. I was healed and would be restored and in this I felt safe as I ventured out into what was for me a new and strange place.

I was able to follow a recipe now and cook without frequent burns, it was time to find recipes I enjoyed and expand my cooking and baking. Prior to being healed I had sold my house and moved into a condominium. I had disposed of everything I didn't need any more, including all my canning supplies. A neighbor started me canning again and yet another friend supplied me with jars and a canner! Little by little these tasks became integrated into my new life.

Setting goals and achieving them had been impossible, now I began to train myself to set long term and short term goals; I needed to clean up my environment, the unfinished projects, fixing and mending, projects to organise and start working on in an orderly fashion, cleaning out an accumulation of paper seeming to pile in on top of me regularly. How then shall I live? This was my focus now – how do I want to live my life, what do I want to accomplish and how will I do it? I had forgotten what "normal" was, the difficulties everyone has that shape the day but don't override it and cause utter chaos. My difficulties had been extreme but controlled by medication meaning I felt emotionally flat, going through the motions of living and functioning. Now I had to learn to cope with the normal ups and downs of life and it took a while.

Friends and neighbours gave me opportunities to be more active and involved in life, encouraging me to engage in some of the activities I had given up.

A neighbor invited me for 18 holes of golf, over forty years since I had played 18 holes, five months pregnant with twins and having trouble swinging through! She assured me I'd be alright; I dragged out my old clubs and off we went. After many years of not being able to do things 18 holes of golf was a daunting prospect but what the heck, I decided to give it a go. Well, everything clicked into place I was still able to shoot a straight ball and even got par on one hole. I was thrilled and surprised and … and …. I did it!!

I used to knit complicated patterns, but all my knitting needles and patterns were gone now but another neighbour gave me a ball of cotton yarn and needles to start me knitting dishcloths, easy and a good place to start.

Exercise had always been a real effort for me but knowing it was important I had the idea to train for a 10K run! I had never been a runner, except for the bus as a child and compulsory Physical Education at school!! A neighbour gave me a board to use for running on the spot and I started, running on the board in my condominium! When I could run on the spot for twenty minutes I tried running outside. I had no proper running shoes or clothes; I wore what I had and kept going. One of my daughters eventually purchased appropriate clothes and I used an old pair of runners from my other daughter. Starting with an online training program for 5K I trained up to 8K and on race day I ran the 10k in a respectable time. What an achievement! It was encouraging after all I had been through.

An avid cyclist moved into our building and put the word out for someone to ride with. I did say I had a bike but had not been riding it and another lady in the building wanted to learn to ride. We got together and with some expert encouragement started exploring our neighborhood and learning how to maintain our bikes. On one of our rides, I experienced happiness for the first time, I was alright, it was wonderful to know the dark night of my life was in the past and there was a bright future for me.

A growing desire to pursue music became a major part of my future plans and that story has its own chapter.

Social interactions were challenging, and I still feel uncomfortable in large groups. This isn't something I need in my life and choose to avoid large group situations whenever possible. I don't need to fight and push through every difficult situation; some are meant to be let go.

It wasn't all progress and plain sailing but little by little the ground under my feet felt more secure and I felt part of life and community once again. My neighbors, friends, and community made a place for me to be me, free from the shackles of mental illness that had kept me in the shadows for too long.

THE GIFT

The ultimate in generosity, in goodness, love.

How do I receive a gift so rare and wonderful?
Thank you seems to pale in light of the greatness of the gift
What I am able to give
Is not enough.

How do I respond?
How do I receive the vastness of this gift?
Give me what I need
to express what is in my heart.
Teach me how to receive this gift
which I have done nothing to earn.

A gift freely given and freely received is the beginning

I receive ……

A SONG IN MY HEART

Music in one form or another has been part of my life since before I started school. At the age of three I took dance lessons, ballet, later tap and then added ballroom. Rhythms and timing were built into me from an early age. At thirteen I applied to join the Sadler's Wells Ballet Company as a student with the blessing of my dance teacher. Successful candidates would board in the City of London, England, at the ballet school and continue academic studies along with dance. Everything was progressing until it was clear I would exceed the ballet company's height limit of 5'6". Those dreams were dashed, and I turned to other pursuits.

My brothers and I were sent off to piano lessons from an early age and every evening it was piano practice for the three of us, my twin brothers and myself. 15minutes, then 20 and 30. I don't remember ever sitting at the piano for longer than 30 minutes, it was a chore to be endured, not a pleasure. However, I did learn enough to give me the basics for future musical endeavours.

As a young teenager, I connected with the local amateur musical theatre group, playing the young characters in their productions and I still have a photograph of me as the crippled boy in the Pied Piper of Hamlin. My mother loved amateur theatre and made sure I was word perfect and could be heard at the back of the theatre. No microphones then, we learned to project our voices and if my voice dropped my mother would raise her hand until I could be heard clearly once again!

In my mid-teens, our Church Girls Brigade, of which I was a member, decided to start a Marching Band. The funds were raised for trumpets and drums; teachers were found, and we became a presentable band for Church Parade (marching from one end of town to church at the other end) one Sunday each month. I learned to play a side drum (snare drum) and the base drum.

By the time I was thirteen I was singing in the adult church choir on Sundays, singing my heart out and thoroughly enjoying it. I sang with the choir until I left home to attend college. I was a member of our Grammar School Choir singing in morning assembly every school day and a focal point of school events. Benjamin Britten Noye's Fludde was a one act opera premiered in the UK in 1958 and has since been staged worldwide. Shortly after the premiere our school performed it, and I was keen to take part; learning to play a bugle I took my place with the orchestra at the back of the assembly hall. The orchestra was seated on the side, stretching from the stage to the back of the hall not in the usual place in front of the stage, and the sound effect was amazing. A wonderful experience.

Commitment to a choir was not possible during the years of building my teaching career, moving to Canada and raising a young family; I was content with church congregational singing once a week. For a while I was able to lead Praise and Worship for the local evening chapter of Women's Aglow, an organization of Christian women and years later when I was able to make the commitment again, I was back in a choir.

There was still a yearning in me to play a musical instrument and a friend offered to lend me a viola and get me started and I subsequently took formal lessons from the principal viola player in our local symphony. I briefly played in the church orchestra but didn't get into it the way I would have liked and never could do a decent job of tuning my instrument. Back to church choirs and my vocal instrument.

Following my manic episode in 1995 and increasing struggles with the illness I lost interest in almost everything, there was no joy to be found anywhere, life was one long struggle to exist. By this time, my children had left home, and I was home alone with my four-legged friend, a wonderful Gordon Setter by the name of Seasac's Deep River, if we were being formal, or Brewster at home!

Yes, my life had deteriorated into a terrible mess on all fronts but there was still a faint flicker of determination to get my life back somehow even though steps backward seemed more numerous than steps forward.

My mother, during the last years of her life was trapped in a body crippled by strokes. I was trapped in a mind crippled by bipolar and cognitive deficits. For my mother, her body would not take her where she wanted to go in the way she wanted. For me, my mind would not do the things I knew full well how to do.

Music was an area of my life I wanted restored, but it seemed like an impossible task because I was depressed and discouraged most of the time. I enjoyed singing as a member of the congregation in the church I was now attending, and several had spoken to me about joining the choir, but I knew much had to change before it was possible. I had to be able to get myself out to choir practice on a regular basis and focus long enough to sing a piece of music from beginning to end. I was still having difficulty focusing on basic daily routines.

Not to be beaten I set about problem solving the issues. I needed a place where I could be somewhat hidden and yet practice singing. A large, non-auditioned community choir presenting concerts twice a year was an excellent starting point. If my mind wandered no one would be affected in a large choir and if I couldn't make it to practice, I wouldn't be missed. I set about working on my focus little by little by bringing my mind back when it wandered off the music score. This was quite easy because I could hear the words the others were singing and get back in at the right place. Gradually my mind wandered less, and my confidence grew. I silently persevered with my mission until I could focus all through a piece of music and stay on track. I had now chalked up a small but significant success in my life. I started to enjoy singing in the choir and was soon ready for a new challenge.

The church choir was much smaller and there was nowhere to hide but it was time to test myself. I went along to choir practice, yes, fearful of trying something new, yes, not sure how it would work out or what I would do if I got stressed and couldn't cope but I went. Stress was overwhelming; my mind froze, and I couldn't always find a safe place to hide.

One lady in the choir took me under her wing, relieving me of the pressure of figuring everything out. She was graciously one step ahead, such a blessing. I survived and thrived rejoicing in the restoration of another part of my life. It was not always plain sailing, there were times when I had to take time out because I couldn't cope but I kept going back. I was afraid of stress, afraid it would take me back to the days when I couldn't tell the time, got lost at the shopping mall and couldn't focus on anything. I ran from it rather than allow it to disable me. When a situation caused me stress, I removed myself, when a relationship caused me stress, I ended it. The approach was isolating but kept me safe.

A Handbell Quartet from Ontario played in church one Sunday in 2005. For me, the visual was as compelling as the sound and as I entered into the music it seemed to flow like dancers. It was amazing and I wanted to do it! After the service, a few of us gathered at the front of the church and the decision was made to somehow start a bell choir. One former member of that quartet had recently moved to Kelowna and although a seasoned ringer had never directed a choir. It didn't take much persuasion to recruit her as our director and we set about the task of acquiring a three-octave set of bells. We secured the blessing of the church and started fundraising. Our director purchased the first three octaves, and fundraising eventually added two more octaves of bells and four octaves of chimes.

In the beginning, playing with the bell choir was manageably difficult for me but as the music pieces became longer and more complex, I began to struggle. I could read music and knew what I was supposed to do but there were times when I couldn't do it and the more I tried, the more stressed I became and the more I struggled. I practiced and practiced but often the practice didn't achieve any improvement at all. My intense discouragement was painful, I was struggling to get my brain to function. It wasn't my fault, my mind wouldn't do what I told it to do, the message frequently did not get through or took longer to activate and the cognitive impairment was worse when my mood was elevated, or I was actively depressed. In fact, my ability to ring bells was a good indicator of where my mood was. The cognitive deficits were, in many ways, more debilitating than the mood swings of bipolar.

I shared these struggles with our director, and she put out an email to her network of ringers seeking ideas for how we could mitigate the effects of my cognitive impairment. The response was most helpful. Enlarge the music so the notes are not as crowded, stay in one position all the time and ring notes easy to locate on the staff with not a lot of fast ringing, use colour coding and marking. I put all this into practice, and it did help tremendously, for a while. Then of course the music got more difficult, my illness escalated, and I struggled again.

Struggling with cognitive issues was something like losing the use of your legs. You know how to walk; you've done all kinds of walking over difficult terrain before, but you can't do it, the capacity isn't there. Mentally. I understood the music, but I couldn't do it. The incredible frustration came from those around me with no framework to understand what was happening and often assumed I didn't know or understand but I did. My mind would not connect to produce the desired result. I tried to listen to all the good advice as graciously as possible knowing most of it did not in any way address the issue I had. I silently struggled through and worked and worked on it at home, often once again with no improvement at all. I frequently could not find a way to make my brain do what I wanted it to do. It had nothing to do with how well educated I was or what I had achieved in the past and everything to do with my brain not responding to the instructions I was giving it.

Much easier to understand physical disabilities but mental challenges are beyond the ability or willingness of most people to understand. Fortunately, our director would say

"I'll leave you to work it out" knowing I would eventually find a way to get it or not!

I'm breaking the silence now hoping it will bring some degree of greater understanding, tolerance and support for individuals suffering with mental illness in whatever form it takes.

During one particularly tough time I was ready to give up but the director of the first quartet I heard sent a message to say, "Don't give up, you enjoy it too much". However, the amount of time I did not enjoy ringing seemed to be increasing but I am grateful I listened to that message and kept going, it didn't become another loss to grieve.

I continued to struggle until the reality of my healing became evident in my music. Practice was resulting in improvement – wow! What a difference! I was eager to improve my bell ringing performance, but I had fallen behind, reduced to playing one bell position consistently, with minimal challenge. I was now anxious to move out of this box my illness had put me in. I spoke to our director and explained I was now obviously healed and would like to try out a different position. Evidently this was not going to be possible, the bell choir had moved on to more difficult music and it was thought I couldn't catch up. I was disappointed. Hurting, I watched as new ringers came in and took positions, I desperately wanted to try but I was not given the opportunity. Perspectives are different and often quite rigid when mental illness is involved. There were those who continued to view me as mentally ill and cognitively impaired long after I was medication and symptom free. The label of "Mental Illness" is hard to remove. There is now a focus on encouraging conversation about mental illness, but society is still too quick to put us in a box, stick a label on and throw away the key!

The door was well and truly closed, but I hadn't come this far to be defeated. One of our ringers who understood what I wanted to do directed a bell choir in a neighboring town and travelled there for practices and performances. I saw an opportunity to catch up and told her I wanted to join her bell choir if she ever needed a ringer.

It was not long before I received an email asking me if I was serious as they were rehearsing music for Christmas and a ringer had dropped out. Within a couple of days, a binder full of music was delivered to me with music for bass and treble positions. I was a member of that bell choir for several months in addition to the choir in my hometown. Encouraged by the director and other choir members I learned all the music and rang performances with them. I played three different positions in the year end concert. What a thrill it was for me.

As I became increasingly secure in the reality of my healing, I thought about ways to increase my musical involvement. I began to consider playing the piano, quite a surprise, as my childhood attempts had been far from enjoyable. However, it was an interesting prospect. I didn't have a piano, only a small keyboard but I decided to try it. Now I've already explained how I was force-fed piano lessons as a child and did not want a repeat, I wanted some gifting to play the piano and I wanted to enjoy it. I was not expecting be a concert pianist in five years!

A member of our bell choir at that time is a piano teacher and I spoke with her about how to get started and thought I might have a lesson occasionally, but my childhood experience was not a memory to encourage me! I quickly realised the keyboard was rather limiting and obtained an acoustic piano that fit my condominium.

I enjoyed playing around with the piano by myself for a couple of months, resisting lessons, fearing they would create pressure, generate stress and it wouldn't be fun anymore. I justified my decision, but knew I would soon reach a limit to how well I could play without lessons. Looking back, it all sounds silly but at the time I was seeing everything through a lifetime of distorted experiences. My healing may have been instant in one sense, but it has been a lengthy process of bringing everything back into right order and the process continues as I encounter new situations and experiences.

Fortunately, the desire to move forward was greater than my fears and off I went for my first lesson, committed to one lesson! I was immediately hooked and now look forward to my lessons, practice is not a chore but an absolute delight. I am grateful for the right teacher, and we can rejoice together in my healing and restoration.

After a few years of learning piano, I met a friends' daughter who was learning the violin. During the visit I played her violin and enjoyed it! I also learned about digital tuners! The wheels started turning and sometime later my son blessed me with a viola for my birthday and another musical adventure began.

Music has always been a cornerstone of my life, through joyous and challenging times. From my early days of dance and piano lessons to my involvement in voice and bell choirs, music has been a constant companion. Despite the struggles with my mental health, I found solace and healing in music. It was through perseverance and the support of people around me that I was able to reclaim this vital part of my life. Today, I am grateful for the journey and the resilience it has instilled in me. As I continue to explore new musical adventures, I am reminded that no matter the obstacles, the melody of life always finds a way to play on.

MY ONGOING JOURNEY

As we move forward, let's embrace new challenges and opportunities with an open heart. Stepping out of our comfort zone to growth and new adventures. Whether it's trying new activities or simply being open to new experiences, the possibilities are endless.

I Look to the Mountains

Across the roof tops
And naked winter trees
The world rests
Quietly patiently
Waiting to spring to life
To bud and blossom again
Fresh white snow
Blankets the world around me
Quietly falling while the world slept
Snow falls sun shines.

I lived under the cloud of mental illness for most of my life, for many years not knowing I had bipolar disorder. No more do I experience the horrors of the ups and downs; no longer do I struggle to live.

I once had a difficult conversation with one of my granddaughters and at the end of the conversation her maturity surprised me when she asked, "So what have we achieved by this conversation?" So, what has my life achieved? What have the lessons taught me? What would I do differently? Where will I go from here? What have I achieved in writing this book? Why have I written the book?

The voice of mental illness needs to be heard, and for those of us who have the experience it is painfully difficult to give our struggles a voice. Writing this book was unbearable at times and I frequently took long breaks thinking I couldn't go on. I don't always get it right; I haven't always made the right choices. What I have written is from my perspective, the way I felt, my reflections, perceptions, and experiences, hoping it will be an encouragement and bring hope to someone. Everyone experiences mental illness in their own way, perspectives and struggles are different, but we all seek to be heard and respected. Perhaps having read this book your mind and heart will be opened to places you've never been before; perhaps the whole picture will be a little less scary; perhaps you will have the courage not to run away from mental illness but walk alongside it when it crashes into your life.

I've recounted a lot of pain and gloom in order to give voice to what goes on in the mind and heart of a person with mental illness. The feelings frequently hidden by the mask we wear socially to try and fit in, to be accepted. I have documented my journey to offer insight and support for others navigating similar paths.

Each chapter of my life brought new challenges and fleeting triumphs, but through it all, I learned the importance of resilience and self-compassion. Engaging in psychiatric therapy provided me with tools to manage my bipolar disorder more effectively. While the road ahead remained uncertain, I tried to hold on to the belief that each day brought an opportunity for growth and healing.

I was able to walk away from bipolar illness into a very different life and I can now choose how to view the past and what to take into the future. Not hiding in denial but walking in the truth which brings life rather than the negative things which result in death. Home was not always a safe place for me when I was growing up and the consequences have caused a great deal of turmoil and pain over the years. However I want to remember the good times, the positive, I want to take the memories of those things into the future. I've grieved what I've lost and let it go because as my friend Liedy always says, "there is no future in my past".

Looking back, I understand how my struggles shaped me into a person capable of enduring and appreciating the complexities of life. This strength has propelled me forward, and as I continue to seek wellness, I remain committed to supporting others in their journeys. Together, we can find light even in the darkest of times.

Throughout these pages, I've explored the challenges and triumphs of healing and personal growth. I've shown how self-awareness is a powerful tool in overcoming obstacles, and resilience and problem-solving skills are essential in navigating life's difficulties.

Maintaining a positive outlook, even in the face of adversity, has been a recurring theme. Difficult times are a part of life, but finding joy in the little things and looking for the silver lining can make all the difference. Expressing gratitude for the support from friends and community has also been a key aspect of this journey. Their encouragement and love have helped me regain confidence and engage in activities that bring me happiness.

No matter what challenges come our way, we can continue to seek the strength within us to overcome them as we are able. The path to healing and growth for each individual is unique and is walked at our own pace. There are things I would like to have done differently but didn't because I couldn't. I can recall situations where help would have made a difference to outcomes, but for any number of reasons, I wasn't able to access the help.

I know I am exactly where I'm supposed to be with all I need, as I need it. I had become so caught up in my fears for the future and my inability to sort it out, I was obsessed with the wrong things. Now I have my priorities straight, I have peace in knowing everything will work out, not perfect but manageable.

I can't catch up on the lost years. I can only let it go and live the life I have today. I choose to spend a great deal of time alone, and time is now filled with activities bringing me great joy. I'm free to choose what social events I attend and I'm comfortable declining invitations not right for me. My musical involvement provides plenty of healthy, enjoyable social connections and I have a small group of friends whose company I value and enjoy.

However you respond to what I've shared, I trust the reading changes you in a positive way allowing you to feel your feelings and let the process achieve its work in you.

Cups And Saucers

just as the plates
and cups, saucers
and glasses have a place in my cupboard
so must the vessels of my life.

to shower, to eat, to work, to shop....
all have a place in my life.

but what about me....
what about the inside of me....

it is from inside of me I grow
it is from inside of me I change....

where are the vessels of my life?
do they have a place?
do I use them often?
or are they buried beneath the
clutter of daily living?

where are they?
are they being used?

my vessels are empty and dry,
covered with dust,
distorted by misuse.

can they be restored
can life come again,
into my empty vessels?

play, fun and laughter
stories...... imagination
adventure, new pursuits,
books, journals,
change, growth,
reckless joy,
a rose,
a fish in the pond,
climbing a tower........

as the vessels are filled again
the beauty of what they contain
shines like a sunset
against the lingering clouds.

POEMS

www.ingramcontent.com/pod-product-compliance
Lightning Source LLC
LaVergne TN
LVHW022223200926
848481LV00006B/2088
9781069856906